AMERICA'S VISION VS. GOD'S STANDARD OF JUSTICE

RETHINKING THE AMERICAN DREAM

Walt Thrun

WALT THRUN

CrossBooks™
A Division of LifeWay
1663 Liberty Drive
Bloomington, IN 47403
www.crossbooks.com
Phone: 1-866-879-0502

© 2014 Walt Thrun. All rights reserved.

No part of this book may be reproduced, stored in a retrieval system, or transmitted by any means without the written permission of the author.

Scripture taken from the New King James Version. Copyright 1979, 1980, 1982 by Thomas Nelson, inc. Used by permission. All rights reserved.

Scriptures taken from the Holy Bible, New International Version®, NIV®. Copyright © 1973, 1978, 1984, 2011 by Biblica, Inc.™ Used by permission of Zondervan. All rights reserved worldwide. www.zondervan.com The "NIV" and "New International Version" are trademarks registered in the United States Patent and Trademark Office by Biblica, Inc.™ All rights reserved.

Scripture quotations taken from the New American Standard Bible®, Copyright © 1960, 1962, 1963, 1968, 1971, 1972, 1973, 1975, 1977, 1995 by The Lockman Foundation. Used by permission." (www.Lockman.org)

First published by CrossBooks   04/28/2014

ISBN: 978-1-4627-3665-2 (sc)
ISBN: 978-1-4627-3666-9 (e)

Library of Congress Control Number: 2014907296

Printed in the United States of America.

This book is printed on acid-free paper.

Any people depicted in stock imagery provided by Thinkstock are models, and such images are being used for illustrative purposes only. Certain stock imagery © Thinkstock.

Because of the dynamic nature of the Internet, any web addresses or links contained in this book may have changed since publication and may no longer be valid. The views expressed in this work are solely those of the author and do not necessarily reflect the views of the publisher, and the publisher hereby disclaims any responsibility for them.

Acknowledgment

In appreciation of Burle and Darlene for providing the most beautiful and serene facility on Table Rock Lake to work on this project.

CONTENTS

1 **Perspectives and Benchmarks** 1

   Inasmuch as the majority of Americans still believe this country is a Christian nation, the Christian perspective is described as well as the benchmark for performance for a Christian nation which is the Bible. Then the Bible is validated as the benchmark.

2 **Israel: Model for the Nations** 12

   The Bible presents Israel as the recipient of God's favor and thus the nation to receive God's standards for righteousness and justice, i.e. the oracles of God. The Bible states that all other nations would look to Israel to observe the blessings for a nation under God.

   This chapter also introduces the two sons of Abraham and the promises given to each.

3 **America's Church – Is the Bride 'Making Herself Ready?'** 48

   This chapter examines the church today in America and compares it to its original purpose and mission.

4   Is God Mocking 'American Exceptionalism'? 90

This chapter examines numerous contemporary issues including partiality in America's judicial system and legislative actions that protect those who break God's laws. Also anti-Biblical fiscal policies including redistribution, deficit spending, and international borrowing will be examined along with partisan politics including liberalism, conservatism, progressivism, and Tea Party ideology and compare such ideologies to Biblical standards.

America as a nation appears to be mocking God; the truth is that God might be mocking America's confidence in herself.

5   Dealing with Contemporary Pharisees 165

Jesus strongly denounced the doctrines of the Pharisees and Sadducees during His earthly ministry. Pharisees were steeped in self-righteousness, hypocrisy, and political correctness while the Sadducees sought relentlessly to suppress speaking the truth.

The argument will be presented that such doctrines represent the underlying causes of America's dysfunctional government today.

6   The Fertile Crescent: Geographic Center of Prophecy 188

This chapter examines in detail the ultimate fulfillment of the promises made to Abraham's two sons, Isaac and Ishmael. The area where Noah and his sons settled after the flood will be the same area where Isaac and Ishmael will finally end their conflict.

Both Islamic literature and the Bible present the nation of Turkey as being profoundly involved in the latter days of this age.

While America believes that establishing democracies in Middle East nations will solve all problems in the area, the Bible presents quite a different perspective.

This chapter also confirms that America's priorities are totally naïve relative to the big picture.

7 Glimpses of the Future 211

This chapter addresses the issue of whether or not America is to play a part in the grand future of the nations according to the Bible.

The term 'future' in this summary chapter includes events in this current age, prophesied events to take place during the tribulation as well as future events in the millennial kingdom and age of ages.

A key issue addressed in this book is whether America is aligning herself with pre-written history, or is preoccupied with current self-serving issues.

CHAPTER 1

PERSPECTIVES AND BENCHMARKS

IT IS WIDELY accepted that everyone has a perspective on life, death, everything in between, and beyond. One's overall perspective will define their value system and serve to interpret events.

Organizations also have perspectives. Such perspectives are typically outlined in an organization's charter or mission statement.

For example one of President Obama's former chiefs of staff contended that Fox News Channel was not really a news organization but was rather an organization that offered a specific perspective on current events.

In this case Fox was described as an organization that focused on the conservative viewpoint. Of course there are other 'news agencies' that focus on a more liberal perspective. It is always interesting to listen to FNC and MSNBC discuss the same issues such as presidential effectiveness, climate change, health care, etc.

Nations have perspectives. America's perspective is broadly expressed in the constitution. Within nations there are often factions, or sects, each with their own culture or ideology.

As would be expected, factions or sects within a nation will produce division. In many nations religious or ideological differences result in civil unrest that may lead to sectarian violence. In America, however, such differences will more often lead to what is termed political gridlock.

Choosing a Perspective

Inasmuch as nearly 8 out of 10 Americans claim to be Christian, this book will examine the Christian perspective and see how that viewpoint defines one's interpretation of issues and events.

America as a constitutional republic is unique. America is a 'free country' where each individual, faction, or sect can still choose their own perspective and view life accordingly, at least for the time being.

Varied and competing perspectives are accompanied and in fact driven by their respective ideologies. Several contemporary and competing perspectives active in America today in addition to Christianity include but not limited to atheism, Buddhism, Hinduism, Judaism, secularism, Islamism, universalism, conservatism, and liberalism. Whatever 'ism' is desired determines its own meaning of events, circumstances, and life itself.

The Benchmark for the Christian Perspective

In order to assess the success or failure of America's Christian perspective there must be a benchmark, or a standard against which to measure performance.

The argument will be presented that such a benchmark is described in great detail in the Bible. There will be those who argue that the Bible focuses initially on the nation of Israel and then the 'church' and, therefore, its applicability is limited to those specific segments of mankind. That viewpoint, however, is extremely myopic.

While the Bible, especially the Old Testament, is largely the history of Israel, their history is unique in that the majority of it was written in advance and confirmed as history became reality. This unique aspect of Israel's history should by itself authenticate the Bible to the whole world.

The New Testament confirms and fulfills the Old Testament and continues the seamless presentation of how selected segments of mankind can and will regain the innocence lost in the Garden of Eden. True, God originally revealed His standard of righteousness and justice to the nation of Israel; however, Israel was chosen to be the living example for all nations both religiously and politically.

The New Testament Apostle and author Paul addressed the applicability of the New Testament based on the Old.

"For whatever things were written before were written for our learning, that we through the patience and comfort of the Scriptures might have hope." Romans 15:4

Paul later confirmed in the New Testament that Israel was and still is God's chosen nation to be an example for all nations. Israel was also chosen to receive the oracles of God.

"What advantage then has the Jew...Much in every way! Chiefly because to them were committed the oracles of God." Romans 3:1-2

The Apostle Paul expanded the argument for those who would limit the applicability of Old Testament teachings to the Old Testament time frame. Writing to the New Testament Church at Corinth, Paul reminded them of the significance of events that happened during Israel's rich history.

"Now all these things happened to them as examples, and they were written for our admonition, upon whom the ends of the ages have come. Therefore let him who thinks he stands take heed lest he fall." 1 Corinthians 10:11-12

The above passage will be referenced numerous times in following chapters.

Confirming Biblical Credibility

The Bible is the most popular book of all time with an estimated printing and distribution of 6 billion copies. The Bible outlines the battle of good vs. evil and provides details of the final outcome of that universal battle.

The Bible was written over a period of 1500 years ending in the first century AD by more than three dozen inspired writers. And even though the Bible has numerous writers and covers a lengthy time span it presents a seamless presentation of man's beginning, present, and future.

The Bible is accepted by Christians as the infallible word of God and contains no abrogation of any kind. The contention that any of the Bible's contents has been corrupted over time is absurd. While the Old Testament was written primarily to and for the benefit of the Jews, the New Testament was written for all peoples of the earth.

"There is neither Jew nor Greek, there is neither slave nor free, there is neither male nor female; for you are all one in Christ Jesus." Galatians 3:28

God has, however, given all mankind freedom of choice to accept the Bible as the word of God or to reject it. In addition the constitution of this great nation provides everyone the freedom to practice any and all religions whether or not they accept the Bible as the infallible word of God.

Why is the Bible the most popular book in history? Many read the Bible for more than religious or spiritual reasons. Many read the Bible to gain knowledge due to its infallibility regarding prophetic fulfillment not only as it relates to Israel, but for many other issues such as the rise and fall of gentile world powers. In other words, many search the Bible purely for knowledge reasons.

While wisdom can be defined as understanding the Bible by way of spiritual insight which is, according to the Bible, a gift from God, knowledge is defined as 'knowing something with familiarity gained through experience or association' i.e. cognizance.

Knowledge is attained and deals primarily with the physical and is acquired through the senses. Wisdom on the other hand is a more holistic view that considers the very reason for existence itself. Overall, the pursuit of knowledge generally precedes the desire for, or even the recognition of, wisdom.

There was a young physicist who was steeped in knowledge but did not have the desire for nor see the need for wisdom. He was totally engulfed in the physical which focused on observable facts and relationships. However, when that young man held his first newborn child in his arms he realized that knowledge was a wonderful thing but it couldn't explain the miracle of life that he was holding and beholding. He then confessed that he was ready to ask for wisdom.

While those with wisdom accept the contents of the Bible by faith, those with knowledge accept the contents of the Bible based on observable facts. Therefore, some knowledge seekers will place much confidence in the Bible because one of the Bible's major and unique features is its ability to establish history and record it before it happens. The Bible is the only book in the world that can claim that feature.

So then, the Bible has proven beyond question to be a credible source book for knowledge seekers as well as for the spiritually enlightened.

The Bible contains literally hundreds of prophecies that are yet to be fulfilled and its readers can have the same level of confidence in those events coming to pass as those innumerable prophecies that have already been fulfilled. Such prophecies address such contemporary issues as the future of Israel, specific prophecies relating to other Mid East nations, the future of democracy, the future of world trade and capitalism, and a host of other significant contemporary issues.

It has been estimated that knowledge doubles every 1½ to 2 years and that period decreases with every generation. Thus the Bible provides the ability to double knowledge in a much shorter time period.

And in addition to wisdom being far superior to knowledge, it is also free.

"If any of you lacks wisdom, let him ask of God...and it will be given to him." James 1:5

God's Standard of Justice and Righteousness Unchanged

The New Testament reveals that when Jesus appeared on earth He confirmed God's standard of justice and righteousness introduced in the Old Testament. In fact Jesus was the primary object of the Old Testament. Very early in His earthly ministry, Jesus explained His relationship to Old Testament law.

"Do not think that I came to destroy the Law or the Prophets. I did not come to destroy but to fulfill. For assuredly, I say to you, till heaven and earth pass away, one jot or one tittle will be no means pass from the law till all is fulfilled." Matthew 5:17-18

Therefore, Jesus confirmed the applicability of God's standard of justice and righteousness revealed to national Israel via Moses 1500 years earlier.

Recall the story Jesus told about the rich man and Lazarus. Both died and the rich man went to Hades where he was suffering while Lazarus was said to be resting in Abraham's bosom. The story continues by telling that the rich man implored Abraham to send Lazarus to warn the rich man's brothers of the torment he was experiencing in Hades. Abraham's response confirmed the immutability and applicability of the original law given in the Old Testament.

"Abraham said to him, 'They have Moses and the prophets; let them hear them.' And he said, 'No, father Abraham; but if one goes to them from the dead they will repent.' But he (Abraham) said to him, 'If they do not hear Moses and the prophets, neither will they be persuaded though one rise from the dead.'" Luke 16:29-31

Jesus was explaining that the spirit and intent of the Mosaic Law was still relevant and there was no excusing the rich man being in Hades because he willfully neglected the original law and oracles of God. That original law was also sufficient warning to his brothers.

In the epistles the Apostle Paul stressed the authenticity of the Scriptures.

"All Scripture is given by inspiration of God, and is profitable for doctrine, for reproof, for correction, for instruction in righteousness..." 2 Timothy 3:16

Notice Paul's statement begins with the word 'all'. Biblical writers penned their messages under God's sovereign inspiration and all scripture should be used as a benchmark for God's immutable standard of justice and righteousness during this current age.

It is interesting that the Apostle Peter quoted and thus reaffirmed the Old Testament prophet Isaiah relative to the applicability and longevity of God's word.

"...The grass withers, and its flower falls away, but the word of the LORD endures forever." 1 Peter 1:24b-25a

Likewise the New Testament ends with a warning similar to the Old Testament warning relative to adding to or subtracting from God's word.

"For I (Jesus) testify to everyone who hears the words of the prophecy of this book: If anyone adds to these things, God will add to him the plagues that are written in this book, and if anyone takes away from the words of the book of this prophecy, God shall take away his part from the Tree of Life..." Revelation 22:18-19

Thus God's standard of righteousness and justice has remained absolutely unchanged for 3500 years and such standard will be/is the benchmark by which America will be evaluated and judged.

Such contemporary thinking that the benchmark should continue to evolve as does morality is totally unfounded. Progressivism is man's attempt to justify present day morality regardless of Biblical standards. The concept of progressivism contends that change is inevitable and, therefore, must be considered in our judicial system. The Bible addresses that ideology.

"For I am the LORD, I do not change...yet from the days of your fathers you have gone away from My ordinances and have not kept them. Return to Me, and I will return to you..." Malachi 3:6-7

The above passage was written approximately 1000 years after the law was given. The Israelites, however, were judged according to that original set of ordinances. The New Testament echoes the concept of the immutability of God's standard of justice and righteousness.

"Jesus Christ is the same yesterday, today, and forever. Do not be carried about with various and strange doctrines..." Hebrews 13:8-9

The term 'various' in the above translates from the Greek *poikilos* meaning many and diverse while 'strange' means doctrines foreign to Christian faith, unheard of, causing surprise and wonder.

The Bible clearly reveals that God the Father and Jesus the Son are immutable and thus do not change. The Father has established His standard of righteousness and the Son will judge mankind in the future based on that same standard.

"...but now (God) commands all men everywhere to repent, because He has appointed a day on which He will judge the world in righteousness by the Man whom He has ordained. He has given assurance of this to all by raising Him from the dead." Acts 17:30-31

Therefore, according to the Bible God raised Jesus from the grave to judge mankind at the appointed time in the future using the standard established thousands of years ago. Therefore, on what basis can principles of our constitution established just hundreds of years ago and based on Biblical principles be updated?

It appears that the only things changing are contemporary societal norms and some contemporary politicians would have us believe the answer is to update our laws to keep pace with such changes.

The wisest man in the world said:

"...Do not associate with those given to change; for their calamity will rise suddenly..." Proverbs 24:21b-22a

So the argument continues. There are many who espouse the concept of applying justice in accordance with changing societal norms and there are those who remain steadfast on believing that judicial administration should be based on the original constitution which was drafted around Biblical principles.

The concept of a living constitution is inconsistent with the Biblical teaching of the immutability of the Godhead and the original definition of righteousness.

There are professed Christians who espouse liberalism and there are many who espouse conservatism. It is always constructive for the individual Christian to examine their political ideology to see if it aligns with Biblical teachings. The Bible is not silent on such issues.

"A good tree cannot bear bad fruit, nor can a bad tree bear good fruit...Therefore by their fruits you will know them." Matthew 7:18-20

Wise King Solomon had some words for those who thought their wisdom was superior to God's standards.

"There is a way that seems right to a man, but its end is the way of death." Proverbs 14:12

Man still has the freedom to choose God's way or his own way as did the Israelites.

America as a nation has that same freedom and is in fact exercising that freedom daily.

CHAPTER TWO

ISRAEL: MODEL FOR THE NATIONS

MAN WAS CREATED perfect in the very image of God. Adam was given a help mate named Eve who was deceived by Satan.

The Bible attributes several names to Satan including but not limited to the following:

"...He laid hold of the dragon, that serpent of old, who is the Devil and Satan..." Revelation 20:2

Several other Biblical names for Satan include deceiver, perverted one, lawless one, imitator, rebel, accuser of the brethren, adversary, Beelzebub, Belial, Lucifer, father of lies, and murderer.

After Satan's deception in the Garden of Eden he, Adam and Eve, and the entire earth were cursed.

Satan would in the future be overcome by the very Seed of the woman whom he had deceived.

"Because you have done this, you are cursed...And I will put enmity between you and the woman, and between your seed and her Seed; He shall bruise your head, and you shall bruise His heel." Genesis 3:14a, 15

Adam and Eve were expelled from the Garden; however, God had replaced their self made covering of leaves with animal skins.

The announcement of the future Seed of the woman and the fact that God had provided covering of animal skins for Adam and Eve were the first hints that God's plan of redemption and restoration had begun.

Many events took place in the next several thousand years. Man was given much freedom to try to govern himself but failed miserably. This issue will be addressed in more detail in chapter 6.

"Then the LORD saw that the wickedness of man was great in the earth, and that every intent of the thoughts of his heart was only evil continually...So the LORD said, 'I will destroy man whom I have created from the face of the earth...' But Noah found grace in the eyes of the LORD." Genesis 6:5, 7-8

And so it was, Noah, his wife, and their three sons, Shem, Ham, and Japheth and their wives were spared to repopulate the earth.

"So He (God) destroyed all living things which were on the face of the ground; both man and cattle, creeping thing and bird of the air. They were destroyed from the earth. Only Noah and those who were with him in the ark remained alive." Genesis 7:23

After the waters subsided Noah's sons settled in an area surrounding the eastern borders of the Mediterranean Sea.

Descendents of Noah's son Shem settled primarily in areas presently known as southwestern Turkey, Syria, and southern Iraq near the intersection of the Tigris and Euphrates rivers.

Shem begot Arphaxad who begot Salah who begot Eber who begot Peleg who begot Reu who begot Serug who begot Nahor who begot Terah who begot Abram (Abraham). The name of Abraham's wife was Sarai whose name was later changed to Sarah.

God's Call to Abraham

God was ready for the next step in His redemptive plan and Abraham was to play a key role in this plan. Recall in the southeast portion of the Fertile Crescent was the city of Ur of the Chaldeans. This is where God initially spoke to Abraham in approximately 2050 BC.

"Now the LORD had said to Abram: 'Get out of your country, from your family and from your father's house, to a land that I will show you.'" Genesis 12:1

After instructing Abraham to leave his native land, God revealed His purpose for him.

"I will make you a great nation; I will bless you and make your name great; and you shall be a blessing. I will bless those who bless you, and I will curse him who curses you; and in you all the families of the earth shall be blessed." Genesis 12:2-3

And so it was, Abraham obeyed the voice of God. It was Abraham's faith in and obedience to God's word that qualified him to be the head of the family that would provide the 'Seed' of the woman who would defeat the great deceiver introduced in the Garden of Eden.

"So Abraham departed as the LORD had spoken to him...Abraham was seventy-five years old when he departed from Haran. Then Abraham took Sarah...and all their possessions... and they departed to go to the land of Canaan." Genesis 12:4-5

God encouraged Abraham as He continued to reveal His plan of redemption for all mankind beginning with a new nation which would subsequently be called 'Israel'.

"After these things the word of the LORD came to Abraham in a vision, saying, 'Do not be afraid, Abraham. I am your shield, your exceedingly great reward.'" Genesis 15:1

Then God revealed the boundaries of the land that Abraham and his descendants would be given.

"...the LORD made a covenant with Abraham, saying: 'To your descendants I have given this land, from the river of Egypt to the great river, the River Euphrates.'" Genesis 15:18

Prophecy foretold and history confirmed that the promises made to Abraham and his descendants would apply and benefit all peoples of the earth in addition to the nation of Israel.

"And behold, the word of the LORD came to him (Abraham), saying, 'Look now toward heaven, and count the stars if you are able to number them.' And He said to him, 'So shall your descendants be.' And he believed in the LORD, and He accounted it to him for righteousness." Genesis 15:4-6

All future blessings from that time forward would be based on taking God at His word; things visible and invisible.

Abraham had two sons who would both play major parts in Israel's history. The two sons will also play a significant part in the future of not only Israel, but the whole world.

God's Promises to Abraham's Sons

The word 'promise' in the Biblical context is a legal term meaning to graciously do or give something. In other words a promise is a unilateral commitment made voluntarily; not the result of negotiations.

God made an extensive promise to Ishmael, the son of Abraham through Hagar.

"Then the Angel of the LORD said to her (Hagar), 'I will multiply your descendants exceedingly, so that they shall not be counted for multitude... Behold, you are with child, and you shall bear a son. You shall call his name Ishmael, because the LORD has heard your affliction. He shall be a wild man; his hand shall be against every man, and every man's hand against him. And he shall dwell in the presence of all his brethren.'" Genesis 16:10-12

The Hebrew for 'wild' translates to a wild donkey, or onager. Such were very aggressive and independent. Onagers were further described by God in the Book of Job.

"Who set the wild donkey free? Who loosed the bonds of the onager, whose home I have made the wilderness, and barren land his dwelling? He scorns the tumult of the city; he does not heed the shouts of the driver. The range of the mountains is his pasture..." Job 39:5-7

God then spoke to Abraham and confirmed that Ishmael would be the beginning of a great nation.

"And as for Ishmael, I have heard you. Behold, I have blessed him, and will make him fruitful, and will multiply him exceedingly. He shall beget twelve princes, and I will make him a great nation." Genesis 17:20

When Hagar and Ishmael were 'cast out' from the presence of Abraham and Sarah, Abraham was given the reason for the promise made to Ishmael.

"Yet I will also make a nation of the son of the bondwoman, because he is your seed." Genesis 21:13

Ishmael and his descendants would be the beginning of the Arab nations.

"Now this is the genealogy of Ishmael, Abraham's son, whom Hagar the Egyptian, Sarah's maidservant, bore to Abraham...Nebajoth; then Kedar, Adbeel, Mibsam, Mishma, Dumah, Massa, Hadar, Tema, Jetur, Naphish, and Kedemah. These were the sons of Ishmael... twelve princes according to their nations." Genesis 25:12-16

The Bible explicitly explains that the promise to Ishmael is totally different than the promise to Isaac. God revealed the following to Abraham relative to Sarah and their future son Isaac that she would bear.

"And I will bless her and also give you a son by her; then I will bless her, and she shall be a mother of nations; kings of peoples shall be from her." Genesis 17:16

It was at this point that Abraham laughed at God's word inasmuch as Abraham was 100 years old and Sarah was 90. Abraham suggested that his son Ishmael already born of Hagar be the heir of the covenant.

"Then God said: 'No, Sarah your wife shall bear you a son, and you shall call his name Isaac; I will establish My covenant with him for an everlasting covenant, and with his descendants after him.'" Genesis 17:19

The different promises made to Isaac and Ishmael defines the two basic categories of all mankind.

The son born of the flesh (Ishmael) represents the attempt to obtain salvation by works while the son of promise (Isaac) represents the attainment of salvation by faith.

"For what does the Scripture say? Abraham believed God, and it was accounted (imputed, credited) to him for righteousness." Romans 4:3

"Therefore we conclude that a man is justified (declared righteous) by faith apart from the deeds of the law." Romans 3:28

Israel - God's Glory Forever

The immutable covenant that God made with Abraham was passed down through Abraham's son Isaac and subsequently passed down to Isaac's son Jacob.

Recall that Jacob wrestled with the Angel of the LORD at Peniel and the Angel of the LORD changed Jacob's name to Israel.

"Then Jacob was left alone; and a Man wrestled with him until the dawn. Now when He saw that He did not prevail against him, He touched the socket of his hip; and the socket of Jacob's hip was out of joint as He wrestled with him. And He said, 'Let Me go, for the day breaks.' But he said, 'I will not let You go unless You bless me!' So He said to him, 'What is your name?' He said, 'Jacob.' And He

said, 'Your name shall no longer be called Jacob, but Israel (Prince with God); for you have struggled with God and with men, and have prevailed.'" Genesis 32:24-28

The significance of this event and the result was summarized by Isaiah more than a dozen centuries later.

"But you, Israel; are My servant, Jacob whom I have chosen, the descendants of Abraham My friend." Isaiah 41:8

Jacob had twelve sons one of whom was named Joseph. Joseph's brothers were jealous of him. Subsequently Joseph's brothers sold him to a company of Ishmaelites who were on their way to Egypt when he was just a teenager.

"Come and let us sell him to the Ishmaelites, and let not our hand be upon him, for he is our brother and our flesh... so the brothers...sold him to the Ishmaelites for twenty shekels of silver. And they took Joseph to Egypt." Genesis 37:27-28

Many years later when Jacob was old, he learned that his son Joseph was alive and an official of Egypt and Jacob desired to see him before his death.

"So Jacob (Israel) took his journey with all that he had, and came to Beersheba, and offered sacrifices to the God of his father Isaac. Then God spoke to Israel in the visions of the night, and said, 'Jacob, Jacob!' And he said, 'Here I am.' So He said, 'I am God, the God of your father; do not fear to go down to Egypt, for I will make of you a great nation there. I will go down with you to Egypt, and I will also surely bring you up again....'" Genesis 46:1-4

Jacob did travel to Egypt as instructed by the LORD and reconciled with Joseph and his other sons. Just prior to Jacob's death he said:

"Gather together and hear, you sons of Jacob, and listen to Israel your father." Genesis 49:1

It was at this time that Jacob proclaimed that his son Judah was God's chosen to perpetuate the Abrahamic covenant.

"Judah, you are he whom your brothers shall praise; your hand shall be on the neck of your enemies; your father's children shall bow down before you. Judah is a lion's whelp; from the prey, my son, you have gone up. He bows down, he lies down as a lion; and as a lion, who shall rouse him? The scepter shall not depart from Judah, nor a lawgiver from between his feet, until Shiloh comes, and to Him shall be the obedience of the people." Genesis 49:8-10

After four centuries of enslavement in Egypt, God called Moses to go to Pharaoh to rescue the Israelites. Moses lacked self-confidence in handling Pharaoh so God told him what to say.

"Then you shall say to Pharaoh, 'Thus says the LORD: Israel is My son, My firstborn. So I say to you, let My son go that he may serve Me. But if you refuse to let him go, indeed I will kill your son, your firstborn.'" Exodus 4:22-23

Israel was called God's firstborn son signifying Israel's preeminence among all nations.

Just three months after the Exodus God addressed Moses at Sinai.

"And Moses went up to God, and the LORD called to him from the mountain, saying, 'Thus you shall say to the

house of Jacob, and tell the children of Israel: You have seen what I did to the Egyptians, and how I bore you on eagles' wings and brought you to Myself. Now therefore, if you will indeed obey My voice and keep My covenant, then you shall be a special treasure to Me above all people; for all the earth is Mine. And you shall be to Me a kingdom of priests and a holy nation.' These are the words which you shall speak to the children of Israel." Exodus 19:3-6

However, shortly after Israel's freedom from their Egyptian enslavement, they begin to rebel against the very one who delivered them.

Recall the Israelites molded a golden calf while Moses was with God at Horeb. Moses reacted by smashing the stone tablets on which God had written His commandments with His own finger.

Moses subsequently interceded for his people and God relented from His threat to destroy the Israelites. Moses recounted that experience to the Israelites before they entered Canaan.

"At that time the LORD said to me (Moses), 'Hew for yourself two tablets of stone like the first, and come up to Me on the mountain and make yourself an ark of wood. And I will write on the tablets the words that were on the first tablets, which you broke; and you shall put them in the ark.'" Deuteronomy 10:1-2

God in His mercy gave Israel a second chance but their restoration was in no way based on their own merits, but rather to vindicate God's own words.

"...that He (God) may fulfill the word which the LORD swore to your fathers, to Abraham, Isaac, and Jacob.

Therefore understand that the LORD your God is not giving you this good land to possess because of your righteousness, for you are a stiff-necked people." Deuteronomy 9:5-6

Then Moses reiterated God's requirements for His standard of righteousness.

"And now, Israel, what does the LORD your God require of you, but to fear the LORD your God, to walk in all His ways and to love Him, to serve the LORD your God with all your heart and with all your soul, and to keep the commandments of the LORD and His statutes which I command you today for your good? Indeed heaven and the highest heavens belong to the LORD your God, also the earth with all that is in it. The LORD delighted only in your fathers, to love them; and He chose their descendants after them, you above all peoples, as it is this day." Deuteronomy 10:12-15

And then nearly forty years later just prior to entering Canaan, God confirmed Israel as His chosen.

"For you are a holy people to the LORD your God; the LORD your God has chosen you to be a people for Himself, a special treasure above all the peoples on the face of the earth. The LORD did not set His love on you nor choose you because you were more in number than any other people, for you were the least of all peoples; but because the LORD loves you, and because He would keep the oath which He swore to your fathers, the LORD has brought you out with a mighty hand, and redeemed you from the house of bondage, from the hand of Pharaoh king of Egypt." Deuteronomy 7:6-8

Then also just prior to entering Canaan, God gave Israel the choice to obey or rebel.

"Now it shall come to pass, if you diligently obey the voice of the LORD your God, to observe carefully all His commandments which I command you today, that the LORD your God will set you high above all nations of the earth." Deuteronomy 28:1

Note the significant 'all'. Notice also the confirmation of Israel being above all nations of the earth if they would choose to obey. Several of the blessings for obedience are listed below.

"The LORD will cause your enemies who rise against you to be defeated before your face..." Deuteronomy 28:7a

Israel would be safe from any who would seek to harm them in the new land.

"The LORD will command the blessing on you in your storehouses and in all to which you set your hand, and He will bless you in the land which the LORD your God is giving you." Deuteronomy 28:8

Israel would be provided with abundance of food and all their endeavors would be blessed. God reminded them that He was giving them the new land.

"Then all the peoples of the earth shall see that you are called by the name of the LORD, and they shall be afraid of you." Deuteronomy 28:10

All the people of the earth would see that the new nation of Israel was the 'Apple of God's Eye' and fear them.

"And the LORD will grant you plenty of goods, in the fruit of your body, in the increase of your livestock, and in

the produce of your ground, in the land of which the LORD swore to your fathers to give you." Deuteronomy 28:11

God would increase the population of the fledgling nation as well as increase their livestock. God would bless them with abundant harvests.

"The LORD will open to you His good treasure, the heavens, to give you rain to your land in its season, and to bless all the work of your hand. You shall lend to many nations, but you shall not borrow." Deuteronomy 28:12

God would bless the new nation with rain as needed to guarantee successful harvests.

The latter part of this verse is especially significant. If Israel would obey God they would have great abundance which would place them in a position of a lender to other nations, but they were not to borrow from other nations.

"And the LORD will make you the head and not the tail; you shall be above only, and not be beneath..." Deuteronomy 28:13a

The new nation would be the example and leader of other nations, and would not be under subjection to any other nation.

"So you shall not turn aside from any of the words which I command you this day, to the right or the left; to go after other gods to serve them." Deuteronomy 28:14

The Israelites were to place their total confidence in their God. God's word was absolute and not subject to compromise. Israel was not to go after other gods, i.e. nothing was to be more important to them than to serve the One and only God.

But there was the other side of Israel's freedom of choice.

"But it shall come to pass, if you do not obey the voice of the LORD your God, to observe carefully all His commandments and His statutes which I command you today, that all these curses will come upon you and overtake you..." Deuteronomy 28:15

God then describes the curses that would befall Israel for disobedience in the same level of detail as He described the blessings for obedience.

"The LORD will send on you cursing, confusion, and rebuke in all that you set your hand to do, until you are destroyed and until you perish quickly, because of the wickedness of your doings in which you have forsaken Me." Deuteronomy 28:20

Israel would be destroyed if they forsook God's instructions and attempted to go it on their own. All their efforts would end in confusion.

"The LORD will change the rain of your land to powder and dust; from the heaven it shall come down on you until you are destroyed." Deuteronomy 28:24

Disobedience would result in devastating droughts. It would be directly the LORD's doing.

"The LORD will cause you to be defeated before your enemies..." Deuteronomy 28:25a

The LORD would lift His hand of protection from the new nation and let their enemies have their way with them.

"The alien who is among you shall rise higher and higher above you, and you shall come down lower and lower. He shall lend to you, but you shall not lend to him; he shall be the head, and you shall be the tail." Deuteronomy 28:43-44

God warned Israel that disobedience would result in extreme degradation in the sight of all around them. God would use multiculturalism to bring them down. Israel would be subject to the aliens among them, and of particular interest is that Israel would become a borrowing nation instead of a lending nation.

Many people in this generation express relief that things are different today than in the days of the Old Testament. They express gratitude that today's God is gentler and more accommodating. Perhaps they should review Paul's teaching.

"Now all these things happened to them as examples, and they were written for our admonition, upon whom the ends of the ages have come. Therefore let him who thinks he stands take heed lest he fall." 1 Corinthians 1:11-12

History reveals that Israel disobeyed God in nearly every way; however, God's covenant was immutable and Israel would be God's glory forever, but not without chastisement along the way.

Approximately seven centuries after entering Canaan, after the time of the judges, and shortly after the nation was divided into northern and southern kingdoms, the prophet Isaiah reminded the southern kingdom of Judah of God's mercy to keep His covenant.

Isaiah began by reminding Judah that God was responsible for the northern kingdom of Israel's chastisement because of their disobedience.

"Who gave Jacob for plunder, and Israel to the robbers? Was it not the LORD, He against whom we have sinned? For they would not walk in His ways, nor were they obedient to

His law. Therefore He has poured on him the fury of His anger and the strength of battle; it has set him on fire all around, yet he did not know; and it burned him, yet he did not take it to heart." Isaiah 42:24-25

And then He began to tell them of God's mercy and plan of redemption.

"But now, thus says the LORD, who created you, 'O Jacob, and He who formed you, O Israel: Fear not, for I have redeemed you; I have called you by your name; you are Mine...Everyone who is called by My name, whom I have created for My glory; I have formed him, yes, I have made him...you are My witnesses, says the LORD, and My servant whom I have chosen, that you may know and believe Me, and understand that I am He. Before Me there was no God formed, nor shall there be after Me...I have declared and saved, I have proclaimed, and there was no foreign god among you; therefore you are My witnesses, says the LORD, that I am God...This people I have formed for Myself; they shall declare My praise.'" Isaiah 43:1, 7, 10, 12, 21

This passage confirms that God created, formed, redeemed, and claimed Israel as His own. Significantly God proclaims that He created Jacob (Israel) for His glory (honor, majesty, esteem). God further confirmed that He chose Israel to be His witnesses to all the earth that He was God. The passage concludes that Israel was formed for His purpose to declare His praise.

Isaiah then proclaims to the whole earth that God has redeemed Jacob (Israel) and glorified Himself in Israel.

"Sing, O heavens, for the LORD has done it! Shout, you lower parts of the earth; break forth into singing, you mountains, O forest, and every tree in it! For the LORD has redeemed Jacob, and glorified Himself in Israel." Isaiah 44:23

The prophet Isaiah subsequently foretold of Israel's prosperity and blessings forever.

"Your sun shall no longer go down...for the LORD will be your everlasting light...Also your people shall all be righteous; they shall inherit the land forever, the branch of My planting, the work of My hands, that I may be glorified." Isaiah 60:20-21

Thus it is seen that Israel was, is, and forever will be the 'Apple of God's Eye'.

Not withstanding Israel was given specific instructions time and again to reflect God's standard of righteousness and justice for a nation.

This standard is the same benchmark by which all nations will be judged, including America.

The following sections will reflect a portion of that standard of conduct for a nation.

God Warned Israel of Multiculturalism

The Bible leaves no doubt that Israel was, is and always will be God's chosen nation and serves as an example for all other nations.

Recall that God promised to make Israel a great nation and further promised them specific land between the Mediterranean Sea and the Euphrates River.

He initially went on before the Israelites to dispossess the inhabitants of the Promised Land Canaan.

"When the LORD your God brings you into the land which you go to possess, and has cast out many nations before you...you shall conquer them..." Deuteronomy 7:1-2

In addition, God gave the Israelites instructions as to how to remain pure and maintain their greatness. The key was to look to God for guidance and to reject any other influence.

"You shall make no covenant with them...They shall not dwell in your land, lest they make you sin against Me. For if you serve their gods, it will surely be a snare to you." Exodus 23:32-33

The word 'snare' means entrapment.

Just prior to the Israelites crossing the Jordan to possess the land of Canaan after the 40 years wandering in the wilderness, the LORD gave Moses more specific details about dispossessing the people who were occupying the land. The Israelites were to completely rid the land of anyone or anything that could negatively influence them in their new home or cause the Israelites to take their eyes off their God.

"Now the LORD spoke to Moses in the plains of Moab by the Jordan, across from Jericho, saying, 'Speak to the children of Israel, and say to them: When you have crossed the Jordan into the land of Canaan, then you shall drive out all the inhabitants of the land from before you, destroy all their engraved stones, destroy all their molded images, and demolish all their high places...'" Numbers 33:50-52

God also made it very clear that all inhabitants of Israel's promised land, whether Jew or alien would be under the jurisdiction of one common law.

For example, specific instructions were given as to who could partake in the religious feast of the Passover.

"And if a stranger dwells among you, and would keep the LORD's Passover, he must do so according to the rite of the Passover and according to its ceremony; you shall have one ordinance (statute), both for the stranger and the native of the land." Numbers 9:14

Similar instructions were given relative to all Jewish offerings and feasts.

"One ordinance (statute) shall be for you of the assembly and for the stranger who dwells with you, an ordinance forever throughout your generations; as you are, so shall the stranger be before the LORD." Numbers 15:15

The concept of one law was also to apply to civil matters in addition to religious matters.

"You shall have the same law (one standard of justice) for the stranger and for one from your own country; for I am the LORD your God." Leviticus 24:22

And then God warned Israel of the consequences of not obeying His instructions to completely rid the land of any religion, culture, or ideology contrary to His prescribed instructions.

"But if you do not drive out the inhabitants of the land from before you, then it shall be that those whom you let remain shall be irritants in your eyes and thorns in your sides, and they shall harass you in the land where you dwell." Numbers 33:55

Well Israel disobeyed God's specific instructions. They did not completely purge the land of all 'anti-God' influence. Judgment was inevitable.

"...and I said... 'You shall make no covenant with the inhabitants of this land; you shall tear down their altars'... but you have not obeyed My voice. Why have you done this?" Judges 2:1-2

Israel has, and still is, paying the price. Their multicultural challenge is far from over inasmuch as the land promised to Abraham, Isaac, and Jacob encompasses much more than the geographical area described as Canaan. The land to be possessed by Israel at the appointed time in the future includes portions of present day Jordan, Lebanon, Syria, Saudi Arabia, and Iraq.

The Bible presents multiculturalism as a deterrent to Israel's purity i.e. a compromising, diluting influence. Israel has and is learning that compromising God's instructions is not a viable option.

Recall God uses Israel's history as an example for this present age.

Forgetting can be Deadly

At end of the 40 year journey after the Exodus Moses recounted Israel's experiences and lessons learned during those 40 years.

"Beware that you do not forget the LORD your God by not keeping His commandments, His judgments, and His statutes...lest – when you have eaten and are full, and have built beautiful houses and dwell in them...and your silver and your gold are multiplied...when your heart is

lifted up, and you forget the LORD your God who brought you out of the land of Egypt, from the house of bondage..." Deuteronomy 8:11-14

One of the primary lessons in the above scripture passage is a warning not to forget 'the LORD your God' because it is He who delivered Israel from bondage and promised them great blessings. The meaning of 'forget' translated from Hebrew means much more than just a 'slip of the mind'. Rather it means to be oblivious of/to, from want of attention. Perhaps the most descriptive synonym is neglect. It is a conscious setting aside.

Also in the above passage the term 'lifted up' means self exaltation, haughty, lofty, or presumptuous.

Moses reminded the Israelites that God had tested them in the wilderness by making them humble so they would realize that God was the source of their good fortune. In other words, God provided; the Israelites had not achieved.

"...The LORD your God...who fed you in the wilderness with manna...that He might humble you and that He might test you... then you say in your heart, 'My power and the might of my hand have gained me this wealth.'" Deuteronomy 8:16-17

"And you shall remember the LORD your God, for it is He who gives you power to get wealth..." Deuteronomy 8:18

History confirms that the southern kingdom of Judah chose to disobey as did the northern kingdom. They did not return to God and the consequence was that Jerusalem was flattened and the choicest of the people of Judah were deported to Babylon (present day Iraq) for a period of seventy years.

The Rise and fall of a Great Nation

When Israel was about to enter the promised land of Canaan, God told Moses in advance what the people would do upon entering their new homeland. He instructed Moses to write it down as a lesson for future generations.

"Now therefore, write down this song...and teach it to the children of Israel; put it in their mouths, that this song may be a witness for Me against the children of Israel. When I have brought them to the land flowing with milk and honey...and they have eaten and filled themselves and grown fat, then they will turn to other gods and serve them; and they will provoke Me..." Deuteronomy 31:19-20

Moses did as instructed. He addressed Israel, and in fact the whole world. He began by describing God and his ways as perfect, righteous, and just. Moses referred to God as 'the' Rock.

"Give ear, O heavens, and I will speak; and hear, O earth, the words of my mouth...For I proclaim the name of the LORD: Ascribe greatness to our God. He is the Rock, His work is perfect; for all His ways are justice, A God of truth and without injustice; Righteous and upright is He." Deuteronomy 32:1, 3-4

Moses then proceeded to describe Israel's predicted conduct upon entering Canaan.

"They have corrupted themselves; they are not His children, Because of their blemish: A perverse and crooked generation. Do you thus deal with the LORD, O foolish and

unwise people? Is He not your Father, who bought you? Has He not made you and established you?" Deuteronomy 32:5-6

Moses asks Israel if their forsaking God is the appropriate repayment for what God has done for them by delivering them from the bondage of slavery in Egypt and sustaining them in the wilderness for 40 years. Then he admonishes them to remember the past and apply those lessons to the future.

"Remember the days of old, consider the years of many generations. Ask your father, and he will show you...He found him (Jacob, or Israel) in a desert land...He kept him as the apple of His eye...He made him ride in the heights of the earth, that he might eat the produce of the fields; He made him draw honey from the rock, and oil from the flinty rock..." Deuteronomy 32:7, 10, 13

Moses describes how God cherished and provided for Israel over previous generations. He took Israel from nothing and caused him to 'ride in the heights of the earth.' He miraculously provided for him through the years.

How did Israel respond?

"But Jeshurun (a Hebrew term for upright, a satirical reference to Israel) grew fat and kicked; 'you grew fat, you grew thick, you are obese!' Then he forsook God who made him, and scornfully esteemed the Rock of his salvation." Deuteronomy 32:15

Israel would believe they had attained their own greatness and wealth. They gave God little or no credit for their good fortune. They highhandedly slighted the importance of God as the source of their status and actually forsook Him. The degradation continued.

"They provoked Him to jealousy with foreign gods; with abominations they provoked Him to anger..." Deuteronomy 32:16

So not only would Israel ignore God, they would replace Him with new gods of their own design for their own convenience.

"Of the Rock who begot you, you are unmindful, and have forgotten the God who fathered you." Deuteronomy 32:18

Therefore, what would be God's response when Israel pushed Him aside?

"And when the LORD saw it, He spurned them...and He said: 'I will hide My face from them...for they are a perverse generation, children in whom is no faith. They have provoked Me to jealousy by what is not God; They have moved Me to anger by their foolish idols.'" Deuteronomy 32:19-21

Remember that God's predominant attributes are His holiness, righteousness, and His justness. All disobedience brings consequences. Because of God's very nature He cannot and will not share His glory as outlined in the first commandment.

"You shall have no other gods before Me." Exodus 20:3

God then outlined His required action against Israel.

"I will heap disasters on them...For they are a nation void of counsel, nor is there any understanding in them. Oh, that they were wise...that they understood this, that

they would consider their latter end!" Deuteronomy 32:23, 28-29

"For the LORD will judge His people...He will say: 'Where are their gods, their rock in which they sought refuge?'" Deuteronomy 32:36-37

God taunts Israel. He tells them that while they think they are wise, they are in fact foolish. Then He tells them to rely on their own conceived gods to deliver them in time of trouble. Notice that God refers to Israel's false sense of security as their 'rock' instead of the 'Rock'. Then He reminds them of His sovereignty and majesty.

"Now see that I, even I, am He, and there is no God besides Me...nor is there any who can deliver from My hand...I will render vengeance to My enemies, and repay those who hate Me." Deuteronomy 32:39, 41

Therefore, if in the above scripture passages taken from the Old Testament book of Deuteronomy we replaced any reference to 'Israel' with 'America' it would be interesting to note if any similarities are found. We could then see if any changes in direction are warranted.

Jerusalem, Jerusalem...

While there are numerous domestic issues that have captured America's attention in recent years, there are also many foreign policy issues that should cause great concern. There is none more important than the Jerusalem question. It is one thing for the Palestinian Authority to make ludicrous demands on Israel regarding Jerusalem, however, when our own administration makes demands on Israel relative to Jerusalem, we better take note.

A major current issue relates to the Israelis continuing to build housing units in East Jerusalem. President Obama in his 2013 speech to the United Nations called Israel's actions 'Israel's occupation' of the West Bank. The Palestinians hope to have their capital in East Jerusalem some day.

There is an anti-Israel coalition at work that wants to compel Israel to make concessions to the Palestinians that would include among other things, giving up parts or all of Jerusalem.

Jerusalem is such a sensitive issue that United Nations' Security Council resolutions prevent Jerusalem from being Israel's capital. The recognized capital of Israel is presently Tel Aviv.

Furthermore, the United Nations considers that Israel is illegally occupying parts of Jerusalem.

Can the future of Jerusalem be negotiated among gentile nations or has Jerusalem's history already been written? The Bible is very clear on this issue. God gave the Israelites specific instructions about His expectations when they entered the land He was giving them to possess.

"These are the statutes and judgments which you shall be careful to observe in the land which the LORD God of your fathers is giving you to possess, all the days that you live on the earth. You shall utterly destroy all the places where the nations which you shall dispossess served their gods....And you shall destroy their altars...and burn their wooden images with fire...But you shall seek the place where the LORD your God chooses, out of all your tribes, to put His name for His dwelling place, and there you shall go." Deuteronomy 12:1-3, 5

The latter part of this passage states that God would choose a location within the Promised Land to establish His earthly dwelling place. He would subsequently disclose where this place would be.

One of the psalmists writing during the time of King David recorded where God's chosen dwelling place was located.

"For the LORD has chosen Zion (Jerusalem); He has desired it for His dwelling place: 'This is My resting place forever; Here I will dwell, for I have desired it.'" Psalm 132:13-14

God then confirmed His choice to David's son Solomon.

"And it came to pass, when Solomon had finished building the house of the LORD (in Jerusalem) and the king's house...the LORD appeared to Solomon...and said to him... 'I have consecrated this house which you have built to put My name there forever, and My eyes and My heart will be there perpetually.'" 1 Kings 9:1-3

God subsequently confirmed the significance of Jerusalem to His prophet Ezekiel.

"And He said to me, (Ezekiel) 'Son of man, this is the place of My throne and the place of the soles of My feet, where I will dwell in the midst of the children of Israel forever.'" Ezekiel 43:7

It is difficult to fathom that those who profess Christianity do not take seriously the contents of the Bible when an issue such as Jerusalem is so blatantly clear. One would think that inasmuch as Israel is still the Apple of God's eye and the future of Israel's real capital Jerusalem is so clearly spelled out the United States would be doing everything in her power to befriend Israel and protect her wellbeing. Cozying up to Israel's enemies is not a viable strategy.

And once again this is foolishness to those who do not place confidence in the Bible. Fortunately our nation's freedoms allow, and in fact welcome, dissenting opinions, at least for the time being.

Following the time of the Judges the Israelites wanted out of their theocracy and demanded a king to rule over them. They wanted to be just like all the other nations surrounding them.

Be Careful What You Ask For

Included in Israel's history are many colorful stories that teach timeless lessons. In approximately 1050 BC Israel was ruled by two judges named Joel and Abijah. These two judges were the sons of Samuel who was a very honorable man; however, these two sons didn't take after their father. They took lightly the word of God, sought personal gain, interpreted the law to promote their personal agendas, and even accepted money from special interest groups.

"Now it came to pass when Samuel was old that he made his sons judges over Israel. The name of his firstborn was Joel, and the name of his second, Abijah; they were judges in Beersheba. But his sons did not walk in his ways; they turned aside after dishonest gain, took bribes, and perverted justice." 1 Samuel 8:1-3

Now all of this caused uproar among the people. They went to Samuel to voice their concerns and demanded change! They complained to Samuel that his sons were not fit to rule and things couldn't continue as they were. They demanded that the very way in which they were governed be changed from a theocracy via judges to a king where governance would be vested in one man.

The people were demanding to abandon the role of God in their political lives. They didn't want to be a special people 'under God'; rather they wanted to be like all the other nations.

"Then all the elders of Israel gathered together and came to Samuel... and said to him, 'Look, you are old, and your sons do not walk in your ways. Now make us a king to judge us like all the nations.'" 1 Samuel 8:4-5

This really upset Samuel who inquired of God as to what to do. The reply was that the people were really rejecting God and their demands had nothing to do with Samuel's leadership. The people did not want God to interfere and get in the way of the pursuit of their own goals.

"But the thing displeased Samuel when they said, 'Give us a king to judge us.' So Samuel prayed to the LORD. And the LORD said to Samuel...'They have not rejected you, but they have rejected Me, that I should not reign over them.'" 1 Samuel 8:6-7

Surprisingly, God told Samuel to give the people what they thought they wanted. He told him to let them have their way. He also told Samuel to tell the people exactly what it would be like to be ruled by a king so they would be totally knowledgeable as to what they were getting into and what to expect.

"Heed the voice of the people in all that they say to you...however, you shall solemnly forewarn them, and

show them the behavior of the king who will reign over them." 1 Samuel 8:9

Well, Samuel followed God's instructions and forewarned the people in great detail what it would be like if the changes they asked for were enacted, i.e. if they were ruled by a king. He told them they would lose many freedoms at the expense of supporting the king, his staff, and followers. He warned them that many free enterprises would be taken over by the king and then managed by appointed czars. He further warned them the government would take from those that had and redistribute it for the support of the king's activities.

"So Samuel told all the words of the LORD to the people...'He will appoint captains...to make his weapons of war and equipment...he will take your sons and appoint them for his own chariots...he will take the best of your fields, your vineyards...and give them to his servants. He will take a tenth of your grain and your vintage, and give it to his officers and servants...He will take a tenth of your sheep. And you will be his servants.'" 1 Samuel 8:10-12, 14-15, 17

The people were also forewarned that the day would come when they would be sorry for their demand for 'change' but the LORD would tell them they would have to live with their choices.

"And you will cry out in that day because of your king whom you have chosen for yourselves, and the LORD will not hear you in that day." 1 Samuel 8:18

But the people ignored all the warnings and pressed forward.

"Nevertheless the people refused to obey the voice of Samuel; and they said, 'No, but we will have a king over us, that we also may be like all the nations...'" 1 Samuel 8:19-20

So the people got their king, a man who outwardly made an impressive appearance.

"There was a man of Benjamin...and he had a choice and handsome son whose name was Saul. There was not a more handsome person than he...From his shoulders upward he was taller than any of the people" 1 Samuel 9:1-2

Well, the history of King Saul is well known and can be summarized succinctly in the words God spoke to Saul's successor David through the prophet Nathan.

"But my mercy shall not depart from him (David), as I took it from Saul, whom I removed from before you." 2 Samuel 7:15

Remember the New Testament passage that places this story in perspective.

"Now all these things happened to them as examples, and they were written for our admonition..." 1 Corinthians 10:11

After King Saul was deposed, God choose a Jewish lad from the tribe of Judah to be Israel's king. During David's rule God revealed more of His plan for Israel and the entire world. Speaking through the prophet Nathan:

"Now therefore, thus shall you say to My servant David, 'I took you from the sheepfold, from following the sheep, to be ruler over My people, over Israel... When your days are fulfilled and you rest with your fathers, I will set up

your seed after you, who will come from your body, and I will establish his kingdom. He shall build a house for My name, and I will establish the throne of his kingdom forever. I will be his Father, and he shall be My son. If he commits iniquity, I will chasten him with the rod of men and with the blows of the sons of men. But My mercy shall not depart from him, as I took it from Saul, whom I removed from before you. And your house and your kingdom shall be established forever before you. Your throne shall be established forever.'" 2 Samuel 7:8, 12-16

The above extremely profound Scripture foretells that David's son Solomon would build God's temple and furthermore the monarchy beginning with David would last forever. Notice the word 'seed' that would come from David's own body. This refers back to the promise in the 3rd chapter of Genesis where God told Satan that he would be defeated by the 'Seed of the woman'.

Several hundred years after the time of the kings and the division of Israel into the north and the south, God continued revealing more of the details of His plan of redemption for all nations and peoples through His prophets.

"For unto us a Child is born, unto us a Son is given...of the increase of His government and peace there will be no end, upon the throne of David and over His kingdom, to order it and establish it with judgment and justice from that time forward, even forever. The zeal of the Lord of hosts will perform this." Isaiah 9:6-7

God's Covenant with Israel is Immutable

Throughout all history God's covenant with Israel is not only immutable but totally unilateral. Israel's promise of future blessings would also include them being a unified nation once again. God spoke through His prophet Ezekiel.

"...Thus says the Lord GOD; 'Surely I will take the children of Israel from among the nations, wherever they have gone, and will gather them from every side and bring them into their own land; and I will make them one nation in the land, on the mountains of Israel; and one king shall be king over them all; they shall no longer be two nations, nor shall they ever be divided into two kingdoms again.'" Ezekiel 36:21-22

Ezekiel goes on to further record Israel's future form of government and in fact reveal who will be the eternal king over them. The following passage just confirms the prophecy given to King David approximately three centuries earlier, only in more detail.

"David My servant shall be king over them, and they shall all have one shepherd; they shall also walk in My judgments and observe My statutes, and do them. Then they shall dwell in the land that I have given to Jacob My servant, where your fathers dwelt; and they shall dwell there, they, their children, and their children's children, forever; and My servant David shall be their prince forever. Moreover I will make a covenant of peace with the, and it shall be an everlasting covenant with them; I will establish them and multiply them, and I will set My sanctuary in their midst forevermore. My tabernacle also shall be with them; indeed

I will be their God and they shall be My people. The nations also will know that I, the LORD, sanctify Israel, when My sanctuary is in their midst forevermore." Ezekiel 36:24-28

Note that the promise is given to Jacob's offspring who is a son of Isaac. David is of the tribe of Judah who is also a son of Jacob. The land promised is the same land promised to Abraham and his descendants in the first book of the Bible. When it is stated that David 'shall be their prince forever' it includes David's seed or offspring. Note further that in the future millennial kingdom and throughout all eternity David's seed will rule the nation of Israel and God will establish His throne forever in their midst.

The prophet Jeremiah confirmed the above, however, he did outline the conditions that would need to exist for Israel to lose their status and favor with God.

"Thus says the LORD, who gives the sun for a light by day, the ordinances of the moon and the stars for a light by night, who disturbs the sea, and its waves roar (the LORD of hosts is His name): 'If those ordinances depart from before Me,' says the LORD, 'then the seed of Israel shall also cease from being a nation before Me forever.' Thus says the LORD: 'If heaven above can be measured, and the foundations of the earth searched out beneath, I will also cast off all the seed of Israel for all that they have done, says the LORD.'" Jeremiah 31:35-37

As history progressed the 'Seed of the Woman' and His family tree would be announced and then confirmed.

"Now in the sixth month the angel Gabriel was sent by God to a city of Galilee named Nazareth, to a virgin betrothed to a man whose name was Joseph, of the house

of David...Then the angel said to her, 'Do not be afraid, Mary, for you have found favor with God. And behold, you will conceive in your womb and bring forth a Son and shall call His name JESUS. He will be great, and will be called the Son of the Highest; and the Lord God will give Him the throne of His father David. And He will reign over the house of Jacob forever, and of His kingdom there will be no end.'" Luke 1:26, 30-33

The gospel writer Matthew gave the specific genealogy and lineage of the 'Seed of the Woman'.

"The book of the genealogy of Jesus Christ, the Son of David, the Son of Abraham: Abraham begot Isaac, Isaac begot Jacob, and Jacob begot Judah and his brothers... Salmon begot Boaz by Rahab, Boaz begot Obed by Ruth, Obed begot Jesse, and Jesse begot David the king." Matthew 1:1-2, 5-6

And while many might reason that the Old Testament history of the nation of Israel is irrelevant to the church and current times, such reasoning is the epitome of naiveté.

"For whatever things were written before were written for our learning..." Romans 15:4

And remember Paul's unforgettable and forever relevant teaching to the church at Corinth.

"Now all these things happened to them (Israelites) as examples, and they were written for our admonition, upon whom the ends of the ages have come." 1 Corinthians 10:11

The 'ends of the ages' does in fact mean the present age of the church.

Yes, Israel is indeed the model for all nations. As one compares Israel's history with that of America, it is quickly noted that America as a nation has also forgotten her God.

Sadly America doesn't have the same promise given Israel which is the promise of complete restoration and eternal existence as a nation, i.e. to be God's glory forever.

CHAPTER 3

AMERICA'S CHURCH — IS THE BRIDE 'MAKING HERSELF READY?'

THE AUTHENTICITY OF any religion or ideology is validated only if built on the 'truth'. Truth can be partially defined as 'the unveiled reality lying at the basis of and agreeing with an appearance...'

Men throughout history have desired and searched for the truth. Even Pilate inquired about it cynically when interrogating Jesus.

"Pilate therefore said to Him, 'So You are a king?' Jesus answered, 'You say correctly that I am a king. For this I have been born, and for this I have come into the world, to bear witness to the truth. Every one who is of the truth hears My voice.' Pilate said to Him, 'What is truth?'" John 18:37-38a

In the New Testament 'truth' is from the Greek *Aletheia* which translates to the related nouns surety, and certainty and the accompanying adverbs surely, and certainly. These terms are used interchangeably in the New Testament.

Jesus came into the world to 'bear witness to the truth' i.e. to reveal God.

"And the Word became flesh and dwelt among us, and we beheld His glory, glory as of the only begotten from the Father, full of grace and truth." John 1:14

"And He (Jesus) is the image of the invisible God, the firstborn over all creation...For in Him all the fullness of Deity dwells in bodily form..." Colossians 1:15, 2:9

"Jesus said to him (Thomas), 'I am the way, the truth, and the life; no one comes to the Father, but through Me.'" John 14:6

If then God is revealed in Jesus and Jesus is the Son of God and the truth; any other description of Jesus is by definition a lie and is the spirit of antichrist. This timeless conflict between truth and lies is the essence of the battle between good and evil.

"Who is the liar but the one who denies that Jesus is the Christ? This is the antichrist, the one who denies the Father and the Son. Whoever denies the Son does not have the Father; the one who confesses the Son has the Father also." 1 John 2:22-23

"...He (the devil) ...does not stand in the truth, because there is no truth in him. Whenever he speaks a lie, he speaks from his own nature; for he is a liar, and the father of lies." John 8:44b

The reason that Christianity is constantly under attack is that Satan knows the truth is embedded in the 'church' of which Christ is the Head.

Wherever truth is found, there will also be deception and the deceiver. The deceiver by nature will pretend to be something or someone that he is not. Deceit by definition requires a lie. Jesus warned that such attempted deception will be present throughout the present age.

"And many false prophets will arise, and will mislead many." Matthew 24:11

Any teaching that denies the deity of Christ and the plurality of the Godhead is not Biblical and must be rejected by the Church.

The 'truth' also includes the entire written word of the Bible inasmuch as a majority of the Bible is in essence the biography of Jesus. Note that Jesus is 'the' truth, not merely 'a' truth.

"Jesus therefore was saying... 'If you abide in My word, then you are truly disciples of Mine; and you shall know the truth, and the truth shall make you free.'" John 8:31-32

And most importantly, the sum of the truth is the basis for eternal life.

"And we know that the Son of God has come, and has given us understanding, in order that we might know Him who is true, and we are in Him who is true, in His Son Jesus Christ. This is the true God and eternal life." 1 John 5:20

Christ not only embodies the truth, but also light, life, and good while anti-Christ epitomizes lies, darkness, death, and evil. Everyone must choose one or the other, there is no in-between.

When the term 'anti-Christ' is used many immediately think of the future leader of the doomed empire who will be empowered by Satan himself. But anything contrary to Christ and His teachings represents the spirit of anti-Christ, and according to the Bible, such opposition to Christ is very much alive and active in the world.

"By this you know the Spirit of God: Every spirit that confesses that Jesus Christ has come in the flesh is from God; and every spirit that does not confess Jesus is not from God; and this is the spirit of the antichrist, of which you have heard that it is coming, and now it is already in the world" 1 John 4:2-3

Again, John draws a sharp distinction between those who are of God and truth and those who are of the world with the spirit of error. The deniers by default are of the spirit of anti-Christ. There is no middle ground. Jesus succinctly made that point in the gospel accounts.

"He who is not with Me is against Me; and he who does not gather with Me scatters." Matthew 12:30

Jesus issued instructions on how to acknowledge and honor His authority during this present age in preparation for the future.

"If you love Me, you will keep my commandments." John 14:15

Enter the Kingdom of Heaven

When John the Baptist began his ministry, even before seeing Jesus, his message centered on warning people that God was about to openly intervene in earthly affairs.

"Repent, for the kingdom of heaven is at hand!" Matthew 3:2

And later when John was in prison Jesus explained to His disciples that while John was greater than the Old Testament prophets, he was less than the least in the kingdom of heaven. John only foresaw the kingdom of heaven while the disciples would actually participate in it.

"Truly, I say to you, 'among those born of women there has not arisen anyone greater than John the Baptist; yet he who is least in the kingdom of heaven is greater than he.'" Matthew 11:11

Jesus taught His disciples to pray that God's kingdom would come to rule the earth in His timing.

"Pray, then, in this way: 'Our Father who art in heaven, Hallowed be Thy name. Thy kingdom come. Thy will be done, on earth as it is in heaven.'" Matthew 6:9-10

Many of Jesus' followers, however, thought that Jesus would establish His prophesied kingdom while He was presently on earth. They didn't realize that the 'kingdom' over which Christ would reign would be a Spiritual kingdom to begin with, but would become physical and visible at a later time.

The kingdom that Jesus ushered in during His lifetime is referred to in the Bible as the Kingdom of Heaven, or the Kingdom of God.

"Now having been questioned by the Pharisees as to when the kingdom of God was coming, He answered them and said, 'The kingdom of God is not coming with signs to be observed; nor will they say, Look, here it is! Or, there it is! For behold, the kingdom of Good is in your midst.'" Luke 17:20-21

When Pilate interrogated Jesus as to whether He was King of the Jews Jesus did in fact acknowledge that He was a King but He further stated that His kingdom was presently not of this world.

"Jesus answered, 'My kingdom is not of this world. If My kingdom were of this world, then My servants would be fighting...but as it is, My kingdom is not of this realm.'"
John 18:36

He was subsequently rejected by the Jewish leaders and crucified. Peter writing in his epistles described Jesus as the 'Rock' and he described his followers as living stones in a spiritual house.

"And coming to Him as to a living stone, rejected by men, but choice and precious in the sight of God, you also, as living stones, are being built up as a spiritual house..."
1 Peter 2:4-5

Peter's statement exemplified a statement Jesus made to Peter in the gospel records.

"And I also say to you that you are Peter (Petros, a small stone), and upon this rock (Petra, immovable boulder) I will build My church; and the gates of Hades shall not overpower it." Matthew 16:18

Christ was/is the 'Rock' in both the Old and New Testaments.

"...our fathers were all under the cloud, and all passed through the sea; and all were baptized into Moses in the cloud and in the sea; and all ate the same spiritual food; and all drank the same spiritual drink, for they were drinking from a spiritual rock which followed them; and the rock was Christ." 1 Corinthians 10:1-4

Therefore, the church is the manifestation of the Kingdom of God.

The Church and the Christian Brotherhood

The Christian Brotherhood is likewise the manifestation of the New Testament church.

The concept of Brotherhood was initially referenced in the Bible 3,000 years ago by David in the Psalms as he was depicting the suffering and victory of the future Messiah.

"...They pierced my hands and my feet...But Thou, O Lord, be not far off; O Thou my help, hasten to my assistance...I will tell of Thy name to my brethren..." Psalm 22:16, 19, 22

The Hebrew term for brethren in the Old Testament translates to 'similar' and 'friend'. It is a term of affection. Paul in the New Testament referred to the predestination of the Christian Brotherhood, i.e. the Church.

"For whom He foreknew, He also predestined to become conformed to the image of His Son, that He might be the first-born among many brethren..." Romans 8:29

This powerful verse reveals that all those whom God elected to salvation He also predestined to be conformed to the image of Jesus, His only begotten Son. This is the very essence of the Christian Brotherhood.

The Greek term for brethren in the New Testament is very similar to the Hebrew meaning 'unity' and 'companion', i.e. a fellowship of love.

Interestingly the Apostle John reveals the first time Jesus referred to His disciples as brothers was after His resurrection.

"Jesus said to her (Mary Magdalene), '...go to My brethren, and say to them, I ascend to My Father and your Father, and My God and your God.'"
John 20:17

Jesus will judge all nations when He returns to earth to end the great tribulation on the basis of how each person treated His brethren during His absence.

"But when the Son Man comes in His glory...then He will sit on His glorious throne. And all the nations will be gathered before Him; and He will separate them from one another, as the shepherd separates the sheep from the goats..." Matthew 25:31-32

The sheep will ask Jesus the reason for their favor.

"Then the righteous will answer Him, saying, 'Lord, when did we see You hungry, and feed You, or thirsty, and give You drink? And when did we see You a stranger, and invite You in, or naked, and clothe You? And when did we see You sick, or in prison, and come to You?' And the King will answer and say to them, 'Truly I say to you, to the extent that you did it to one of these brothers of Mine, even the least of them, you did it to Me.'" Matthew 25:37-40

But there is an even greater privilege to being Jesus' brethren; to be Jesus' brethren means also to be children of God the Father.

"So then, brethren...for all who are being led by the Spirit of God, these are sons of God...the Spirit Himself bears witness with our spirit that we are children of God..." Romans 8:12a, 14, 16

The plan was originally revealed in Genesis when God said the 'Seed of the woman' would destroy the enemy, the devil. Paul explained later to the early church how the concept of 'sonship' became reality.

"But when the fullness of the time came, God sent forth His Son, born of a woman, born under the Law, in order

that He might redeem those who were under the Law, that we might receive the adoption as sons." Galatians 4:4-5

And when the Apostle John revealed the incarnation of Christ he included that all who would receive the Son would be granted the status of sonship.

"But as many as received Him, to them He gave the right to become children of God, even to those who believe in His name..." John 1:12

Therefore, the Christian is an adopted child of God and a joint heir with Christ. Such is the highest position for mankind other than Christ Himself in His humanity.

Due to the coveted position of being God's children Christians are and will be subjected to great jealousy and persecution.

Their Father will vigorously deal with their persecutors in His timing.

"Never take your own revenge, beloved, but leave room for the wrath of God, for it is written, 'VENGEANCE IS MINE, I WILL REPAY, SAYS THE LORD.'" Romans 12:19

The Bible has much to say about its defenders and deniers. The Christian Brotherhood has and will continue to be confronted by heretics, infidels, and unbelievers.

The Brotherhood's initial step in its strategy in dealing with heretics and infidels is to take a stand on their Biblical belief system.

"Therefore, my beloved brethren whom I long to see, my joy and crown, so stand firm in the Lord, my beloved." Philippians 4:1

"It was for freedom that Christ set us free; therefore keep standing firm and do not be subject again to a yoke of slavery." Galatians 5:1

The Brotherhood is encouraged to take a stand as did Peter and John relative to speaking about Christ.

"Now as they observed the confidence of Peter and John...they were marveling... 'And now, Lord, take note of their threats, and grant that Thy bond-servants may speak Thy word with all confidence...'" Acts 4:13, 29

After taking the Biblical stand with boldness, the Brotherhood is to rebuke heresies.

The Apostle Paul also addressed the issue boldly.

"I solemnly charge you in the presence of God and of Christ Jesus, who is to judge the living and the dead, and by His appearing and His kingdom: preach the word...reprove, rebuke, exhort, with great patience and instruction. For the time will come when they will not endure sound doctrine..." 2 Timothy 4:1-3

One might think that the Brotherhood's bold stand on Biblical teachings and rebuking those entwined in heresy would provoke enmity. That is absolutely true, but the Bible is also very clear on how the Christian Brotherhood is to handle deniers, i.e. Biblical enemies.

"Blessed are you when men revile you, and persecute you, and say all kinds of evil against you falsely, on account of Me. Rejoice, and be glad, for your reward in heaven is great, for so they persecuted the prophets who were before you." Matthew 5:11-12

"You have heard that it was said, 'YOU SHALL LOVE YOUR NEIGHBOR, and hate your enemy.' But I say to

you, 'love your enemies, and pray for those who persecute you in order that you may be sons of your Father who is in heaven...'" Matthew 5:43-45

Note again the confirmation of sonship for those adhering to Biblical teachings. The Greek base for 'love' for one's enemies in this passage is from *agapao* meaning to be concerned for one's total wellbeing by accepting Biblical truths. It definitely does not translate from the Greek *phileo* which is associated with sharing belief systems or having common interests.

Therefore, while the Christian Brotherhood will be hated and derided for their stand, they are to love those who persecute them by living exemplary lives in the midst of their enemies, thereby, reflecting their faith. The persecutors will experience justice in due time.

"For after all it is only just for God to repay with affliction those who afflict you, and to give relief to you who are afflicted and to us as well when the Lord Jesus shall be revealed from heaven with His mighty angels in flaming fire, dealing out retribution to those who do not know God and to those who do not obey the gospel of our Lord Jesus. And these will pay the penalty of eternal destruction, away from the presence of the Lord..."

2 Thessalonians 1:6-9

There will be times when the Christian Brotherhood will be tempted to exact justice in the current age; however, Christians are never to be incited to violence against those who hate them.

Satan hates what God loves

That Satan hates what God loves may seem obvious, but the implications may be more subtle than they seem. As might be expected Satan hates Christ the Son of God, Christ's followers i.e. the Church, and of course, Israel.

Consider firstly Jesus Himself. God loves His Son, the ultimate 'Seed of the woman'.

"The Father loves the Son, and has given all things into His hand." John 3:35

The purpose of the Son was also announced by the Apostle John.

"...The Son of God appeared for this purpose, that He might destroy the works of the devil." 1 John 3:8b

The enmity between Satan and the Son was originally announced in the Garden of Eden and will come to its conclusion in the future.

And then God loves those who love and trust His Son.

"...for the Father Himself loves you, because you have loved Me, and have believed that I came forth from the Father." John 16:27

Satan's hatred for the believers can be better understood by considering his loss of heavenly authority and being relegated to the less glorious position of 'ruler of this world'.

The Greek base for 'world' is *kosmos* meaning in essence the present earthly order of things as opposed to the kingdom of God. The idea is transience versus permanence. It highlights the focus on the pleasures and enjoyments of this present life. A basic premise is that maximum fulfillment is found during life on earth with little consideration given to eternal life, or the kingdom of God.

Satan tempts mankind to follow their natural instincts and fulfill natural desires. Such a strategy is deceptive and is warned against repeatedly in the Bible. Inasmuch as Christ represents just the opposite, the world and its 'ruler' hate Christ and all of His followers.

"If you were of the world, the world would love its own; but because you are not of the world, but I chose you out of the world, therefore the world hates you." John 15:19

And of course, Satan hates Israel. When God called out the nation of Israel to be a light and example to all nations, He pronounced His love for them.

"The LORD did not set His love on you nor choose you because you were more in number than any of the peoples, for you were the fewest of all peoples, but because the LORD loved you..." Deuteronomy 7:7-8a

Satan has hated Israel from her calling and has attempted to destroy that nation and her future King from the time God set them apart unto this day and will continue his attack until his final demise.

"...And the dragon stood before the woman (Israel) who was about to give birth, so that when she gave birth he might devour her child. And she gave birth to a son, a male child, who is to rule all the nations with a rod of iron..." Revelation 12:4-5

Recall also that King Herod had all male children two years old and younger killed in an attempt to thwart God's plan for Israel and her future king.

God loves those who do His will. Thoughts and actions are either prompted by God or the enemy. The source of every ideology or action can be determined with surprising accuracy.

If it's not truth…what?

A cursory review of the Bible reveals there are perhaps as many references to deceit as there are to truth. That should not be surprising inasmuch as sin and deceit began in the heavens with Lucifer, son of the morning. He couldn't deal with the reality that he was a created being.

"But you said in your heart… 'I will raise my throne above the stars of God…I will ascend above the heights of the clouds, I will make myself like the Most High.'" Isaiah 14:13-14

Having rebelled against his creator, Satan began his career of deceit when God created man in His own image in the Garden of Eden.

Deceit in the scriptures has multiple synonyms such as lie, fraud, trickery, seduce, bait, or guile. Deceit is used to lead one astray, cause to error, or to form a wrong judgment.

All through the ages Satan has been attempting to steer men away from the truth which has been previously defined as God revealed in Jesus the Son. If people believe the lie, they will spend eternity with the deceiver apart from God.

Inasmuch as Jesus is the truth, there is no deceit in Him as confirmed by Peter.

"(Jesus) WHO COMMITTED NO SIN, NOR WAS ANY DECEIT FOUND IN HIS MOUTH…" 1 Peter 2:22

Believers are exhorted not to be deceived.

"...we are no longer to be children, tossed here and there by waves, and carried about by every wind of doctrine, by the trickery of men, by craftiness in deceitful scheming..." Ephesians 4:14

"Little children, let no one deceive you...the one who practices sin is of the devil; for the devil has sinned from the beginning." 1 John 3:7a, 8a

"But false prophets also arose among the people, just as there will also be false teachers among you, who will secretly introduce destructive heresies, even denying the Master who bought them bringing swift destruction upon themselves. And many will follow their sensuality, and because of them the way of the truth will maligned..." 2 Peter 2:1-2

Men are also admonished to not participate in deception.

"Truthful lips will be established forever, but a lying tongue is only for a moment. Deceit is in the heart of those who devise evil...lying lips are an abomination to the LORD, but those who deal faithfully are His delight."
Proverbs 12:19-20, 22

Jesus warned that deception would increase in the latter days.

"For false Christs and false prophets will arise and will show great signs and wonders, so as to mislead, if possible, even the elect." Matthew 24:24

The Bible is once again very succinct. The choice is before every individual, i.e. to believe in and cling to the truth, or deny the truth and accept a lie. Because of the scope of the results of this choice, this decision transcends any other set before man on his pilgrimage on planet earth.

It's the Biblical version of 'Truth or Consequences'.

Cautions for the Church

There are many who believe that inasmuch as we are in the postmodern cultural times the church must change to keep pace with the changing culture. Subscribers to the 'emerging church' movement are concerned that the present church is not capable of attracting or communicating with those in the postmodern cultural era.

As would be expected the movement is gathering wide appeal because it offers a better quality of life to all without addressing the sin question.

There is little question that people can be drawn into a movement that promotes the betterment of social conditions, restores the earth, welcomes a wide variety of philosophies, and doesn't make a big issue of man's basic depravity called sin.

In addition to the 'emerging church' there is a more subtle movement underway involving several mainline denominations in an attempt to bolster sagging attendance as well as to gain new members. Many new and existing churches are embracing contemporary philosophies and miscellaneous activities to provide wide appeal.

Several other titles attached to this effort include the 'new paradigm' church and the 'market-driven' church. The impetus for this movement is that society was changing while the church was not keeping pace. It was felt that something more must be offered. After it was determined what potential members wanted, then a marketing strategy could be developed to make the church more appealing.

A pioneer in the area of church growth was Robert Schuller, who in fact claims to be the founder of the church growth movement. His philosophy was quite simple… "Find out what would impress the non-churched in your community and then offer it to them."

Schuller's thinking was that the major perceived need of people was self-esteem. He then initiated a radical shift from God to human needs as the focus for his church. The results were impressive as his church grew dramatically.

A problem with Schuller's approach is that the recognition and elevation of one's self-esteem is totally contradictory to Biblical teachings. Consider self-esteem is related to pride and is a contradiction to humility and meekness.

There are literally hundreds of scripture references commending humility and meekness and just as many others that condemn pride and self-exaltation.

One of the results is a contemporary gospel that attempts to convince people Christ died to meet their needs. The focus becomes self-centered, i.e. knowing and accepting oneself rather than Christ-centered, i.e. knowing the mission and real purpose of Christ and His death. Sin was redefined from rebellion against God to a flawed strategy to gain fulfillment.

The Biblical gospel has limited appeal to the need fulfillment seeker who is looking for satisfaction here and now. The Bible, however, promises persecution, trials, and discipline in the here and now.

"Then Jesus said to His disciples, 'If any one wishes to come after Me, let him deny himself, and take up his cross, and follow Me. For whoever wishes to save his life shall

lose it; but whoever loses his life for My sake shall find it. For what will a man be profited, if he gains the whole world, and forfeits his soul? Or what will a man give in exchange for his soul?'" Matthew 16:24-26

"And indeed, all who desire to live godly in Christ Jesus will be persecuted." 2 Timothy 3:12

The 'seeker-sensitive' and 'market-driven' churches are motivated more by market research and polls than the word of God. There is the ultimate disparity between the two sources.

Christ Himself described the church as it will appear during the latter days.

"I know your deeds, that you are neither cold nor hot... So because you are lukewarm, and neither hot nor cold, I will spit you out of My mouth. Because you say, 'I am rich, and have become wealthy, and have need of nothing,' and you do not know that you are wretched and miserable and poor and blind and naked...Those whom I love, I reprove and discipline; be zealous therefore, and repent." Revelation 3:15-17, 19

So while the 'seeker-sensitive' and 'market-driven' churches think they have it all together and are in need of nothing, some will actually leave Christ out of the picture and are, therefore, in need of everything.

The latter days of the church age will, however, experience a great loss of members in spite of all the efforts to grow it.

Although the word 'apostasy' is not found in the Bible, its concept is Biblical. The terminology found in the Bible for the concept is 'falling away'. The meaning is renunciation, departure, or abandonment of a religion or a previous loyalty. It is the opposite of taking a stand.

In the present context the Bible states that during the latter days of the church period there will be a great falling away. Informal research has intimated that a large percent of those who consider themselves 'Christian' are really not.

Many, including the Evangelist Billy Graham have estimated the percent of self-proclaimed Christians who are really pretenders to exceed half. The self-proclaimed Christians are subject to apostasy.

Apostasy can and will be traced to many reasons including being deceived by false doctrines or seduced by false teachers.

"But the Spirit explicitly says that in later times some will fall away from the faith, paying attention to deceitful spirits and doctrines of demons..." 1 Timothy 4:1

"Now we request you, brethren, with regard to the coming of our Lord Jesus Christ...Let no one in any way deceive you, for it will not come unless the apostasy comes first, and the man of lawlessness is revealed, the son of destruction." 2 Thessalonians 2:1, 3

During these latter days men will embrace false doctrines and place more significance on political correctness than truth.

Jesus said that only the elect will recognize and reject the deception and hold fast to the truth.

Religious consultant and Pastor Jack McKinney PhD stated on FOX news channel "We're turning God into a monster by teaching of a literal hell." Shortly thereafter a

FNC anchor stated it was nonsense to believe Jesus was the only way to heaven.

Therefore, when it comes to apostasy it might be prudent to pause and evaluate the political and religious climate in America and then ask…are we there yet?

The Bride is subject to Deception

In the Old Testament God illustrated marriage between husband and wife as a permanent relationship by comparing His relationship with Israel.

But there will always be the influence of Satan attempting to deceive the bride who was/is more susceptible to being deceived. It began with Eve.

"For I am jealous for you with a godly jealousy; for I betrothed you to one husband, that to Christ I might present you as a pure virgin. But I am afraid, lest as the serpent deceived Eve by his craftiness, your minds should be led astray…" 2 Corinthians 11:2-3

Eve desired to have something for self fulfillment and gratification that God did not provide.

"When the woman saw that the tree was good for food, and that it was a delight to the eyes, and that the tree was desirable to make one wise, she took from its fruit and ate…" Genesis 3:6

She in fact told the Serpent God had revealed that she would die if she ate of the tree of the knowledge of good and evil. Satan's counter:

"…You surely shall not die!" Genesis 3:4b

Remember how Satan's emissary was described.

"Now the serpent was more crafty (cunning, subtle) than any beast of the field..." Genesis 3:1a

The Hebrew base for 'cunning' and 'subtle' has several synonyms including deceive and lie.

The Biblical teaching of marriage and the temptation of the bride was illustrated with Hosea's wife Gomer who analogically represented Israel.

"...For she said, 'I will go after my lovers, who give me my bread and my water...'" Hosea 2:5b

But Gomer had been deceived.

"And she will pursue her lovers, but she will not overtake them; and she will seek them, but will not find them. Then she will say, 'I will go back to my first husband, for it was better for me then than now!' For she does not know that it was I who gave her the grain, the new wine, and the oil, and lavished on her silver and gold..." Hosea 2:7-8

"...for the land commits flagrant harlotry, forsaking the LORD." Hosea 1:2b

The Hebrew base for 'harlotry' is also translated as adultery, whoredom, apostasy, departure, forsakenness, or to succumb to satanic deception.

As a husband's jealousy is aroused when his wife strays from his protective umbrella, so is God's jealousy over Israel.

"They made Him jealous with strange gods; with abominations they provoked Him to anger... 'They have made Me jealous with what is not God; they have provoked Me to anger with their idols...'" Deuteronomy 32:16, 21

Therefore, harlotry, i.e. spiritual adultery, which is departing from God and His word, is the result of deception by the enemy. The zenith of such folly is described as the 'Mother of Harlots' and will be dealt with appropriately at the end of the current age.

"...The Serpent Deceived Me..."

As mentioned, synonyms for deceive in the Old Testament include lie, beguiled, delude, or to seduce. The meanings of deceive in the New Testament are nearly the same; however, it includes 'to lead away from the truth.'

The truth has been defined as the deity of Christ, the incarnate Son of God.

The Bible reveals that lies and deception were used by the serpent to lead Eve away from the truth. Deception will be found at an increasing rate as the end of this age approaches, along with blasphemy and hypocrisy.

The 'serpent' who deceived Eve is clearly identified in the final book of the Bible.

"And the great dragon was thrown down, the serpent of old who is called the devil and Satan, who deceives the whole world..." Revelation 12:9

Jesus described the devil as the father of lies, i.e. 'there is no truth in him.' Thus Satan's overarching lie is the denial of Christ as the Son of God. Such denial is to reject God's plan of redemption for man.

"Who is the liar but the one who denies that Jesus is the Christ? This is the antichrist, the one who denies the Father and the Son. Whoever denies the Son does not have the Father..." 1 John 2:22-23

Sadly however, many will believe the lie. The Apostle Paul also addressed the issue of deceit, or the rejection of Jesus as the Son of God.

"...that is, the one whose coming is in accord with the activity of Satan, with all power and signs and false wonders, and with all the deception of wickedness for those who perish, because they did not receive the love of the truth so as to be saved. And for this reason God will send upon them a deluding influence so that they might believe what is false..." 2 Thessalonians 2:9-11

In the final book of the Bible it is clearly stated that those who receive the mark of the beast (antichrist) will also believe the lie.

"And the beast was seized, and with him the false prophet who performed the signs in his presence, by which he deceived those who had received the mark of the beast and those who worshiped his image; these two were thrown alive into the lake of fire which burns with brimstone. And the rest were killed with the sword which came from the mouth of Him who sat upon the horse..." Revelation 19:20-21

In the above scripture passage the One who kills those that received the mark of the beast is Christ Himself. The irony is that Christ is the object of Satan's deception which centered on the lie that Jesus wasn't deity. Yet Christ will emerge the victor by defeating not only the one who devised the lie, but also those that believed it.

After the true bride of Christ is taken to the marriage supper of the Lamb the counterfeit, i.e. the harlot, will emerge and prevail for a very short time.

"...Come here, I shall show you the judgment of the great harlot who sits on many waters, with whom the kings of the earth committed acts of immorality, and those who dwell on the earth were made drunk with the wine of her immorality." Revelation 17:1b-2

During one's lifetime, all must address the issue of who Jesus is. That issue is at the heart of the battle of good vs. evil and truth vs. the lie. It will become increasingly difficult to cling to the truth as Satan will exert his total, but restricted, power to perpetuate the lie. The Bible is explicitly clear on the person of Christ as the Son of God, and as the future Judge, King, and Lawgiver over the whole earth.

The Kingdoms of this World

During the present age while the Kingdom of God is spiritual and invisible, the kingdoms of the world are very visible and active, deceiving and enticing. During this age God has given over the rule of the kingdoms of the world to Satan.

The Kingdom of God and the kingdoms of the world once again define the two distinct divisions of all mankind.

"Do not love the world, nor the things in the world. If any one loves the world, the love of the Father is not in him. For all that is in the world, the lust of the flesh and the lust of the eyes and the boastful pride of life, is not from the Father, but is from the world." 1 John 2:15-16

At the beginning of Jesus' earthly ministry Satan tempted Him to avoid the cross by accepting the kingdoms of the world over the Kingdom of God.

"And he (the devil) led Him up and showed Him all the kingdoms of the world in a moment of time. And the devil said to Him, 'I will give You all this domain and its glory; for it has been handed over to me, and I give it to whomever I wish. Therefore if You worship before me, it shall all be Yours.'" Luke 4:5-7

Satan was allowed to tempt (test) Jesus. The Greek base for 'test' in this context means to try one's virtue or to solicit to sin. Of course Jesus replied that only the LORD your God should be worshipped.

Notice that the authority Satan offered Jesus was first delivered (given) to him as part of God's master plan. Any authority or power exercised by Satan or his puppets, the anti-Christ and the false prophet, has been committed to them by God and subject to His sovereign rule.

Jesus acknowledged Satan's delegated authority. He also acknowledged that Satan would soon be judged and would lose his position to the conquering Christ.

"Now judgment is upon this world; now the ruler of this world shall be cast out." John 12:31

Therefore, Jesus is the king of the invisible spiritual kingdom during the church age, while Satan has been given authority over the physical kingdoms of the world during this age.

During the tribulation period Satan will be extremely active as will his two major emissaries.

"And he (John) stood on the sand of the seashore. And I saw a beast coming up out of the sea, having ten horns and seven heads, and on his horns were ten diadems, and on his heads were blasphemous names...And the dragon

gave him his power and his throne and great authority." Revelation 13:1-2

The beast described is the final world kingdom consisting of ten member nations represented and ruled by the anti-Christ having received his authority from Satan. Then another beast also receiving his power from Satan is allowed to appear to assist the first beast.

"And I saw another beast coming up out of the earth; and he had two horns like a lamb, and he spoke as a dragon. And he exercises all the authority of the first beast in his presence. And he makes the earth and those who dwell in it to worship the first beast..." Revelation 13:11-12

Satan's purpose hasn't changed over the ages. He and his accomplices blaspheme God and make desperate attempts to deceive and tempt all mankind who are still on the earth.

At the end of the tribulation period Christ returns and utterly defeats the two beasts.

"And the beast was seized, and with him the false prophet...these two were thrown alive into the lake of fire..." Revelation 19:20

At that time Satan is imprisoned in the bottomless pit (abyss) for a thousand years and the kingdoms of the world become the Kingdom of the Lord.

"And I saw an angel coming down from heaven, having the key of the abyss...and he laid hold of the dragon, the serpent of old...and bound him for a thousand years, and threw him into the abyss...until the thousand years were completed..." Revelation 20:1-3

At the end of the thousand years Satan is released from the bottomless pit only to be quickly defeated after one final attempt to deceive those on the earth.

"And the devil who deceived them was thrown into the lake of fire and brimstone, where the beast and the false prophet are also; and they will be tormented day and night forever and ever." Revelation 20:10

Thus ends the author of evil who attempted to deceive the whole world.

Is 'Chrislam' a Viable Option to Promote World Peace?

A lengthy letter was drafted by Muslim scholars entitled 'A Common Word between Us and You' in 2007 and sent to the Pope and many other world religious leaders. The letter attempted to find common ground between Islam and both Christianity and Judaism. In the summary statement of their letter they state:

"Muslims and Christians together make up well over half of the world's population. Without peace and justice between these two religious communities, there can be no meaningful peace in the world. The future of the world depends on peace between Muslims and Christians."

The context of the title of the Muslim letter is found in Koran 3:64.

"Say: O people of the Scripture! Come to a common word between us and you: that we shall worship none but God (Allah), and that we shall ascribe no partner unto Him…"

Within their lengthy letter the phrases 'and that we shall ascribe no partner unto Him' and 'He hath no associate' are found 15 times. In essence Muslims recognize Jesus as a Messenger of God, but deny His deity. Their letter states:

"Muslims recognize Jesus Christ as the Messiah, not in the same way Christians do (but Christians themselves anyway have never all agreed with each other on Jesus Christ's nature), but in the following way: '...the Messiah Jesus son of Mary is a Messenger of God...'" Koran 4:171

Their letter implies that Christians themselves are divided on the nature of Christ, i.e. whether He is basically a Messenger of God, or in fact deity as the Son of God, as Jesus Himself states, *"I and My Father are one."*

Mary was indeed the mother of Jesus but the Bible clearly states that He is much more than a messenger, i.e. He *"will be called the Son of the Highest."*

"And the angel said to her, 'Do not be afraid, Mary; for you have found favor with God. And behold, you will conceive in your womb, and bear a son, and you shall name Him Jesus. He will be great, and will be called the Son of the Most High; and the Lord God will give Him the throne of His father David; and He will reign over the house of Jacob forever; and His kingdom will have no end." Luke 1:30-33

The issue of Jesus' deity was also a point of contention between Jewish leaders and Jesus during Jesus' time on earth also but was settled abruptly.

"And they (Sanhedrin) all said, 'Are You the Son of God, then?' And He said to them, 'Yes, I am.'" Luke 22:70

Then after Jesus' resurrection His disciples saw Him and He spoke to them saying:

"...All authority has been given to Me in heaven and on earth." Matthew 28:18

Ecumenism Espouses 'Chrislam'

The Yale Center for Faith & Culture in their response to 'A Common Word between Us and You' suggested that Christianity can be reconciled with Islam. The Muslim community and ecumenism agree that world peace can be achieved with such reconciliation.

The Yale response letter began with an apology for the way that Christians have treated Muslims both in the past and presently.

"…Since Jesus Christ says, 'First take the log out of your own eye, and then you will see clearly to take the speck out of your neighbor's eye,' we want to begin by acknowledging that in the past (i.e. in the Crusades) and in the present (e.g. in excesses of the 'war on terror') many Christians have been guilty of sinning against our Muslim neighbors…we ask forgiveness of the All-Merciful One and of the Muslim community around the world."

The Yale apology letter quoted extensively from the first epistle of John.

"The one who does not love does not know God, for God is love." 1 John 4:8

That is a wonderful scripture; however, the thought is incomplete without the verse immediately following (which was not deemed relevant in Yale's letter of apology) inasmuch as the two verses are intrinsically linked.

"By this the love of God was manifested in us, that God has sent His only begotten Son into the world, so that we might live through Him." 1 John 4:9

The Yale letter continued by quoting:

"We love, because He first loved us. If someone says, 'I love God,' and hates his brother, he is a liar; for the one who does not love his brother whom he has seen, cannot love God whom he has not seen?" 1 John 4:19-20

Again, omitted from the Yale response letter were other verses from the same chapter of the same Epistle.

"And we have beheld and bear witness that the Father has sent the Son to be the Savior of the world. Whoever confesses that Jesus is the Son of God, God abides in him, and he in God." 1 John 4:14-15

And in the second chapter of the same epistle, the Apostle John writes:

"Whoever denies the Son does not have the Father; the one who confesses the Son has the Father also." 1 John 2:23

President Obama did say something in his 'new beginning' speech to the world's Muslims in Cairo in 2009 that should be accepted as truth.

"…partnership between America and Islam must be based on what Islam is and not what it isn't."

The more one learns about Christianity and Islam the more prepared one is to take a stand with one or the other.

The response letter by the Yale Center for Faith and Culture is the epitome of political correctness.

Separation of Church and State…Bah! Humbug!

There are those who believe the constitution prescribes the 'separation of church and state'. In reality that premise is based solely on a phrase used by Thomas Jefferson in a letter to the Danbury Baptist Association on January 1, 1802 to assure them that government would not intrude into their affairs. Not only is that premise not included anywhere in this nation's founding documentation, neither is it found in the Bible.

When one hears the terms 'Bah! Humbug'! it connotes something phony, i.e. a hoax or fraud. Therefore, the validity of the premise of the separation of church and state is questionable at best.

During the Christmas season Christians celebrate the birth of Christ and several Old Testament prophecies are highlighted that pointed to the future birth of the coming King and to His future eternal throne.

"For a child will be born to us, a son will be given to us…" Isaiah 9:6a

But that scripture needs to be placed in proper context by considering the remainder of that verse and the one immediately following.

"…And the government will rest on His shoulders; and His name will be called Wonderful Counselor, Mighty God, Eternal Father, Prince of Peace. There will be no end to the increase of His government or of peace, on the throne of David and over his kingdom, to establish it and to uphold it with justice and righteousness from then on and forevermore." Isaiah 9:6-7

Several key and revealing words in the above are government, throne, and kingdom. All three of these words refer to dominion, sovereignty, royal rule, and reign.

"But as for you, Bethlehem Ephrathah, too little to be among the clans of Judah, from you One will go forth for Me to be ruler in Israel." Micah 5:2

This verse not only reveals where Christ would be born, but that He would be the ultimate ruler over Israel.

And as we look forward in scriptures to the prophecy in the Revelation of Jesus Christ it is noted that not only will Jesus rule over Israel forever, but also over all of the nations.

"And I saw heaven opened; and behold, a white horse, and He who sat upon it is called Faithful and True; and in righteousness He judges and wages war...and from His mouth comes a sharp sword, so that with it He may smite the nations; and He will rule them with a rod of iron; and He treads the wine press of the fierce wrath of God, the Almighty." Revelation 19:11, 15

This scripture will be the fulfillment of another 3,000 year old prophecy.

"Ask of Me, and I will surely give the nations as Thine inheritance, and the very ends of the earth as Thy possession. Thou shalt break them with a rod of iron, thou shalt shatter them like earthenware." Psalm 2:8-9

The Bible states clearly that Christ will be the sovereign ruler and king of all nations including Israel beginning with the millennial kingdom. And let it not be forgotten His authority as head of the church.

"...as Christ also is the head of the church...the church is subject to Christ..." Ephesians 5:23-24

The unity of the governance of church and state is fulfilled and exemplified in the description of New Jerusalem.

"And I saw no temple in it, for the Lord God, the Almighty, and the Lamb, are its temple...And the nations shall walk by its light, and the kings of the earth shall bring their glory into it." Revelation 21:22, 24

Therefore, the future unification of the church and state is as sure as the demise of democracy as a form of government.

Supersessionism Never Entered the Mind of God

While supersessionism, or replacement theology, never entered the mind of God, it has, sadly to say, entered the mind of the World Council of Churches.

The general meaning of supersessionism is that the promises God made to Israel will be fulfilled by the church because of Israel's disobedience. In other words, the thinking is that the church has superseded God's favor for the nation of Israel.

The Scriptures, however, succinctly teach that Israel and the Church are separate entities, they will both abide forever, and both have distinctly different purposes and rewards.

They do, however, share several common foundational truths.

Both the church and national Israel were bought and redeemed by the blood of Christ.

Secondly, both the church and the nation of Israel are descendants of Abraham, Isaac, and Jacob and both will be governed eternally through their descendant David, i.e. Christ.

The calling of Abraham was a significant step in God's redemptive plan after the fall of man.

"And I will multiply your descendants as the stars of heaven, and will give your descendants all these lands; and by your descendants all the nations of the earth shall be blessed; because Abraham obeyed Me and kept My charge, My commandments, My statutes and My laws." Genesis 26:4-5

Again, God reiterated that Israel would inherit a homeland and be a blessing to all the nations of the earth. Abraham and his descendants would be a blessing to all because he believed God and took Him at His word.

Shortly thereafter God spoke to Abraham's grandson Jacob.

"And behold, the LORD stood above it (the ladder reaching to heaven) and said, 'I am the LORD, the God of your father Abraham and the God of Isaac; the land on which you lie, I will give it to you and to your descendants. Your descendants shall also be like the dust of the earth... and in you and in your descendants shall all the families of the earth be blessed.'" Genesis 28:13-14

Once again the promise confirmed the land for national Israel and blessings for all the families of the earth.

The promise for an eternal nation of Israel was confirmed and described by the prophet Ezekiel.

"And My servant David will be king over them (united Israel)...And the nations will know that I am the LORD who sanctifies Israel, when My sanctuary is in their midst forever." Ezekiel 37:24a, 28

Note from the above passage the word 'forever'. If that Old Testament promise for national Israel was to be transferred to the church because of Israel's continued disobedience, Jesus would have so stated.

The apostle Matthew described Jesus' instructions as He sent the twelve disciples out to announce the kingdom of heaven.

"These twelve Jesus sent out after instructing them, saying, 'Do not go in the way of the Gentiles, and do not enter any city of the Samaritans; but rather go to the lost sheep of the house of Israel. And as you go, preach, saying, The kingdom of heaven is at hand.'" Matthew 10:5-7

Jesus plainly instructed His disciples at that time not to go preaching to the gentiles, but rather to the Jews.

Matthew subsequently recorded the incident where a gentile woman who had a daughter that was demon possessed begged Jesus for mercy. His disciples advised Him to send her away but the woman persisted.

"But He (Jesus) answered and said, 'I was sent only to the lost sheep of the house of Israel...It is not good to take the children's bread and throw it to the dogs.' But she said, 'Yes, Lord; but even the dogs feed on the crumbs which fall from their master's table.'" Matthew 15:24, 26-27

Jesus once again proclaimed that His priority was to save the lost children of Israel. The woman also acknowledged His saying and realized that she, being a gentile was being referred to as a dog in the above, could partake of the leftover crumbs from the master's table.

Jesus acknowledged her faith and healed her daughter at that very hour.

The immutability of Israel's favor with God is proclaimed repeatedly throughout the epistles.

"For I am not ashamed of the gospel, for it is the power of God for salvation to every one who believes, to the Jew first and also to the Greek." Romans 1:16

In this Scripture passage Paul acknowledges the priority given the Jews but then adds that believing Gentiles can also partake of the plan of salvation.

The Jews were very jealous that the blessings of Abraham would be offered to and shared with the gentiles. The rejection of God's plan of salvation offered by faith and not by works opened the door for the Gentiles.

"And the next Sabbath nearly the whole city assembled to hear the word of God. But when the Jews saw the crowds, they were filled with jealousy, and began contradicting the things spoken by Paul, and were blaspheming. And Paul and Barnabas spoke out boldly and said, 'It was necessary that the word of God should be spoken to you first; since you repudiate it, and judge yourselves unworthy of eternal life, behold, we are turning to the Gentiles.'" Acts 13:44-46

The Jews' rejection was for the purpose of taking the gospel to the Gentiles and was spoken of initially in the Old Testament.

"He says, 'It is too small a thing that You should be My Servant to raise up the tribes of Jacob, and to restore the preserved ones of Israel; I will also make You a light of the

nations so that My salvation may reach to the end of the earth.'" Isaiah 49:6

And even though Paul was a tremendous teacher and preacher to the Gentiles, he was first a Jew and a Pharisee. By man's reasoning Paul should have been the last one on earth to minister to the Gentiles.

"...If anyone else has a mind to put confidence in the flesh, I far more: circumcised the eighth day, of the nation of Israel, of the tribe of Benjamin, a Hebrew of Hebrews; as to the Law, a Pharisee; as to zeal, a persecutor of the church; as to the righteousness which is in the Law, found blameless." Philippians 3:4b-6

Paul never stopped loving the Jews after his calling by Jesus to grow the church and he above all men was inspired to explain God's immutable plan for Israel. He explained Israel's rejection of Jesus as he reinforced God's plan to the Christians in Rome.

"I say then, they did not stumble so as to fall, did they? May it never be! But by their transgression salvation has come to the Gentiles, to make them jealous. Now if their transgression be riches for the world and their failure be riches for the Gentiles, how much more will their fulfillment be!" Romans 11:11-12

Paul emphatically emphasized that Israel's fall (stumbling) was temporary for the benefit of the Gentiles. Then he explained that if their fall was a blessing for the Gentiles, how much more blessing for the world at the time of their future total restoration.

Paul then warns the Gentiles (church) not to boast or be prideful.

"But if some of the branches were broken off, and you, being a wild olive, were grated in among them and became partaker with them of the rich root of the olive tree, do not be arrogant toward the branches; but if you are arrogant, remember that it is not you who supports the root, but the root supports you. You will say then, 'Branches were broken off so that I might be grafted in.' Quite right, they were broken off for their unbelief, and you stand only by your faith. Do not be conceited, but fear; for if God did not spare the natural branches, neither will He spare you." Romans 11:17-21

Paul explains that some Jews rejected salvation and they represent natural branches broken off the tree, or root system. Gentiles were then grafted in the tree. He reminds the church that the root system supports the branches and not the other way around. He then reminds the Gentiles that they being wild branches were grafted in the tree contrary to nature and are subject to be removed if they should boast of their status.

Then Paul summarizes the mystery of Israel's temporary status.

"For I do not want you, brethren, to be uninformed of this mystery, lest you be wise in your own estimation, that a partial hardening has happened to Israel until the fullness of the Gentiles has come in..." Romans 11:25

So much for supersessionism and replacement theology.

Betrothed: Soon to be Wed!

The bride is the New Testament Church and the Bridegroom is Jesus Christ the Son of God. The terms 'wedding' and 'marriage' are synonymous from the Greek *gamos* which means the actual and permanent joining together of husband wife.

The Bible first introduces this concept in the early chapters of Genesis. Adam and Eve were created in the very image of their Creator for the purpose of being joined together as one.

"For this cause a man shall leave his father and his mother, and shall cleave to his wife; and they shall become one flesh." Genesis 2:24

The Hebrew for 'cleave' in the above has several synonyms including join and adhere. Significantly it also means 'to pursue'. The bridegroom pursues his chosen bride.

As noted previously in this chapter the metaphor of the marriage between deity and His chosen was further illustrated with national Israel being the bride and the bridegroom being God the Father.

It all begins with the betrothal, or commitment between the two parties.

"And I will betroth you to Me forever; yes, I will betroth you to Me in righteousness and in justice, in lovingkindness and in compassion, and I will betroth you to Me in faithfulness. Then you will know the LORD." Hosea 2:19-20

According to Jewish tradition the marriage between the bridegroom and the bride occurred in several stages.

The bride was typically selected by the Bridegroom's father with little input from the prospective bride. A price was then paid to the bride's family.

Between the betrothal and the marriage ceremony, the bridegroom would return to His Father's house to prepare a place for the couple to live.

"In My Father's house are many dwelling places; if it were not so, I would have told you; for I go to prepare a place for you. And if I go and prepare a place for you, I will come again, and receive you to Myself; that where I am, there you may be also." John 14:2-3

The Apostle Paul taught that the relationship between God's Son and the Church was a mystery revealed in the present age.

"This mystery is great; but I am speaking with reference to Christ and the church." Ephesians 5:32

A mystery in the Bible is the unveiling of a previously hidden truth to be revealed at the precise timing on God's time span.

Inasmuch as Christ's bride, i.e. the church represents the elect during the present age, and the elect were chosen and written in the Book of Life at the foundation of the world, it can be concluded that the betrothal was also accomplished at the foundation of the world.

Another aspect of the mystery revealed by Paul was the price paid for the bride which was the blood of the Bridegroom.

"Be on guard for yourselves and for all the flock...to shepherd the church of God which He purchased with His own blood." Acts 20:28

The next step in the marriage covenant is for the bridegroom to return for His bride. Most Bible students are in agreement that the return of Christ for His bride is illustrated in the following:

"For the Lord Himself will descend from heaven with a shout, with the voice of the archangel, and with the trumpet of God; and the dead in Christ will rise first. Then we who are alive and remain shall be caught up together with them in the clouds to meet the Lord in the air. And thus we shall always be with the Lord." 1 Thessalonians 4:16-17

The exact timing for this event is also unknown, however, its sequence in the chain of pre-written future events is well known. The 'rapture' according to Scripture occurs prior to the tribulation period.

During the tribulation period, the bride and Bridegroom will be at the center of marriage festivities in the heavens. The festivities will conclude with the marriage supper.

"Let us rejoice and be glad and give the glory to Him, for the marriage of the Lamb has come and His bride has made herself ready...and he said to me, write, 'Blessed are those who are invited to the marriage supper of the Lamb.'" Revelation 19:7, 9

The marriage clearly takes place after the tribulation activities described in the final book in the Bible, i.e. The Revelation of Jesus Christ.

Thus, the bride has definitely 'made herself ready' for the marriage. It should be noted, however, that the bride's readiness has little to do with the personal efforts of the bride but rather must be attributed to the actions of the Bridegroom.

"Husbands, love your wives, just as Christ also loved the church and gave Himself up for her; that He might sanctify

her, having cleansed her by the washing of water with the word, that He might present to Himself the church in all her glory, having no spot or wrinkle or any such thing; but that she should be holy and blameless." Ephesians 5:25-27

Therefore, the plan of God for the New Testament church is right on schedule, in spite of national and internal interferences which attempt to curtail her sanctification. Thus Jesus' teaching that the gates of Hades 'shall not overpower' His bride is confirmed.

National Israel and the New Testament church do have several significant points of commonality. Both are betrothed to their Creator and both were bought with the blood of the Lamb.

CHAPTER 4

IS GOD MOCKING 'AMERICAN EXCEPTIONALISM'?

T HIS CHAPTER WILL examine such issues as fiscal policy, foreign policy, and political ideologies to see how America compares with God's standard of righteousness and justice revealed to national Israel.

Also to be examined will be this nation's administrative, legislative, and judicial branches of government to note the level of resemblance, if any, to Biblical standards.

"Hear now, O Israel, the decrees and laws I am about to teach you. Follow them so that you may live...Do not add to what I command you and do not subtract from it... Observe them carefully, for this will show your wisdom and understanding to the nations, who will hear about all these decrees and say, 'Surely this great nation is a wise and understanding people.'" Deuteronomy 4:1-2, 6

The events recorded in the book of Deuteronomy took place during the 40 years between the Exodus from

Egyptian bondage to just prior to entering the promised land.

The instructions given to the Israelites were/are immutable and were/are to direct the behavior of all nations through the ages.

The Apostle Paul summarized that 40 year period and wrote of its current applicability 1,500 years later.

"These things happened to them as examples and were written down as warnings for us, on whom the fulfillment of the ages has come. So, if you think you are standing firm, be careful that you don't fall!" 1 Corinthians 10:11-12

Our founding fathers attempted to express and incorporate those precepts in the constitution of the United States.

The question is, therefore, has America done any better in obeying those instructions than national Israel to whom these instructions were originally given as an example and model?

I) A Look at America's fiscal policies

Biblically Dissecting the 'Fiscal Cliff'

The term 'fiscal cliff' has been a popular phrase in recent years. The meaning centers on the role of government and how to fund its operation. The cliff represents the resulting consequences if spending and taxing policies are not agreed to and enacted by both the Senate and House of Representatives.

The political ideology of president Obama and shared by the democratically controlled senate centers on increasing revenue to fund government spending by way of tax collection. Taxes are certainly appropriate to fund government; however, the larger question is the role of government.

The primary role of government is defined in Scripture as maintaining law and order based on God's standard of justice.

"Everyone must submit himself to the governing authorities, for there is no authority except that which God has established...For he is God's servant to do you good. But if you do wrong, be afraid, for he does not bear the sword for nothing. He is God's servant, an agent of wrath to bring punishment on the wrongdoer...This is also why you pay taxes..." Romans 13:1-2, 4, 6

The Bible also indicates maintaining a military is sanctioned by God which would require government funding.

"Moses said to the Gadites and Reubenites, 'Shall your countrymen go to war while you sit here?' ...The Gadites and Reubenites said to Moses, 'We your servants will do as our lord commands...your servants, every man armed for battle, will cross over to fight before the LORD, just as our lord says.'" Numbers 32:6, 25-27

In the New Testament Jesus spoke in a parable of the consequence of not funding the required military.

"Or suppose a king is about to go to war against another king. Will he not first sit down and consider whether he is able with ten thousand men to oppose the one coming against him with twenty thousand? If he is not able, he will

send a delegation while the other is still a long way off and will ask for terms of peace." Luke 14:31-32

Additionally the Bible describes wars that will be waged in the future. Therefore, taxes are sanctioned to administer law and order plus maintain an adequate military presence.

Presently, however, some believe that government should have a much larger role in the lives of the citizenry.

Proponents of larger government participation believe that government should be a provider of benefits and services in addition to those sanctioned in the Bible. Each additional proposed benefit and service can be weighed against scriptural precepts.

The epitome of depravity is when government funds are used to protect those who break God's laws. While some such additional government services are obviously anti-scriptural, others are more subtle.

One of the more subtle anti-scriptural ideologies held by the Obama administration is termed 'the protection of the middle class'. In essence the meaning is equalization of the nation's wealth among all citizens which is accomplished by redistribution. That is a flagrant attempt to usurp God's authority.

"But remember the LORD your God, for it is he who gives you the ability to produce wealth..." Deuteronomy 8:18a

The attempt to provide more anti-scriptural benefits and services to citizens can lead to much more serious problems. If there is a revenue shortfall and deficit spending is required, a government must resort to borrowing.

The Bible is quick to point out that one of the curses for a nation that disobeys God's word is for that nation to be a borrower while blessings for a nation that obeys God's words is to be a lender nation. In addition:

"...and the borrower is servant to the lender." Proverbs 22:7b

Interestingly there are those at both ends of the political spectrum who claim membership in the Christian Brotherhood. That is confusing inasmuch as there are many who claim to be Christians who espouse contemporary ideologies contrary to Biblical teachings. Jesus shed light on such inconsistencies.

"By their fruit you will recognize them...A good tree cannot bear bad fruit, and a bad tree cannot bear good fruit." Matthew 7:16a, 18

Therefore, the fiscal issues facing this nation can be evaluated to see if they are in sync with Biblical teachings.

Every individual has the freedom to choose whether to take the Bible seriously or dismiss it if they hold the conviction that politics and Scripture should not be intermingled.

The Real American Idol

While the majority of Americans believe this country is still the greatest and most blessed nation on earth an increasing number are beginning to wonder if our priorities are misguided. Most in the executive branch of government, and in fact a large percentage of Americans, believe that a strong economy should be this nation's top priority. Such thinking is not new.

Preparing for the 1992 presidential election democratic strategist James Carville initiated the slogan, 'It's the economy, stupid!' That strategy propelled Bill Clinton into office and ousted George Bush senior from office after one term.

Immediately after the horrendous attack on the World Trade Center in 2001, then president George W. Bush stated that the strength and resiliency of the American people would be measured by how quickly the stock market would be up and running. America has made economic prowess her idol.

The Bible has much to say about idols, other gods, and money. Firstly, the first two commandments specifically address the issues of other gods and idols. The Hebrew word for idol translates as deficient, worthless, vain, and/or empty. There is God and then there are gods. They must be differentiated.

"For great is the LORD and most worthy of praise; he is to be feared above all gods. For all the gods of the nations are idols..." Psalm 96:4-5

"But the LORD is the true God; he is the living God, the eternal King. When he is angry, the earth trembles; the nations cannot endure his wrath. Tell them this: 'These gods, who did not make the heavens and the earth, will perish from the earth and from under the heavens.'" Jeremiah 10:10-11

Thus gods and idols are inseparable and are defined as vanity or emptiness. Likewise God and wisdom are inseparable.

"I, wisdom, dwell together with prudence...Counsel and sound judgment are mine...By me kings reign and rulers make laws that are just...I walk in the way of righteousness... The LORD brought me forth as the first of his works...I was appointed from eternity...Blessed are those who keep my ways...For whoever finds me finds life and receives favor from the LORD." Proverbs 8:12, 14-15, 20, 22-23, 32, 35

One may, therefore, choose gods and idols or God and wisdom, but not both. They are not compatible.

Now let's inject the subject of the economy, or money.

Solomon addressed the issue in his writings.

"Wisdom is a shelter as money is a shelter, but the advantage of knowledge is this: that wisdom preserves the life of its possessor." Ecclesiastes 7:12

The Hebrew word for shelter translates to protection. Solomon said that a person can choose to rely on money or wisdom and then he proclaims the superiority of wisdom. He continues with a more detailed example of relying on money.

"Woe to you, O land whose king was a servant...If a man is lazy, the rafters sag; if his hands are idle, the house leaks. A feast is made for laughter, and wine makes life merry, but money is the answer for everything." Ecclesiastes 16a, 18-19

In this satirical example Solomon states than an immature ruler believes that more money, i.e. revenue or taxes can cover the consequences of an inept administration.

The issues of idols and money are also addressed in the New Testament.

"...keep yourselves from idols." 1 John 5:21

The Greek for idols translates into a false god or an imaginary deity whether or not intended as a representative of the true God. So not unlike the Old Testament, idols and false gods are to be avoided. They are not compatible with God and wisdom. Jesus voiced that concept of incompatibility.

"No one can serve two masters. Either he will hate the one and love the other, or he will be devoted to the one and despise the other. You cannot serve both God and Money." Matthew 6:24

The Apostle Paul when writing to Timothy also warned about idolizing money:

"For the love of money is a root of all kinds of evil. Some people, eager for money, have wandered from the faith and pierced themselves with many griefs." 1 Timothy 6:10

There are some very basic Biblical tests to see if we as a nation are pursuing fiscal policies that will be blessed by God.

"If you fully obey the LORD your God and carefully follow all his commands...The LORD will open the heavens, the storehouse of his bounty, to send rain on your land in season and to bless all the work of your hands. You will lend to many nations but will borrow from none." Deuteronomy 28:1, 12

America, like Israel, may choose obedience or disobedience.

"However, if you do not obey the LORD your God and do not carefully follow all his commands...The alien who lives among you will rise above you higher and higher, but you will sink lower and lower. He will lend to you, but you

will not lend to him. He will be the head, but you will be the tail." Deuteronomy 28: 15, 43-44

As of late 2013 the United States was indebted in the amount of $2.4 trillion to just China and Japan. It appears as if we are pursuing gods and idols instead of God and wisdom.

II) Evaluating America's Judicial System

A Model for our Judicial System

As Israel prepared to enter the promised land of Canaan Moses reviewed what was expected of them.

"In the fortieth year...Moses proclaimed to the Israelites all that the LORD had commanded him concerning them." Deuteronomy 1:3

Note Israel's expectations were based on obedience to commandments issued by their sovereign God.

The instructions given to the Israelites included the requirements of their judicial system.

"Appoint judges and officials for each of your tribes in every town the LORD your God is giving you, and they shall judge the people fairly. Do not pervert justice or show partiality. Do not accept a bribe...Follow justice and justice alone, so that you may live and possess the land the LORD your God is giving you." Deuteronomy 16:18-20

There are several points that stand out. Firstly, the future land of Israel is a gift from God. The only requirement of the Israelites was/will be their obedience to the Giver. The Israelites were to judge all matters justly without bias. And very importantly, the benchmark for judgment or true justice was God's commandments which constituted their law.

The above passage is strikingly clear. For a judge to show partiality or to take a bribe would pervert justice. Partiality is shown when a judge considers other factors associated with either party rather than limit the judgment to the facts of the issue being judged.

A bribe is another tactic used to influence impartial judgment and if Israel allowed such tactics the result would be their temporary expulsion from the land promised to them.

However, because the covenant with Abraham was unconditional and immutable Israel will someday in the future permanently possess all the land promised to them approximately four thousand years ago.

In America today the ultimate benchmark defining what is 'right' is the constitution which was originally intended to reflect God's standard of justice.

Bribes flourish through the affects of lobbying, i.e. the quid pro quo factor.

Concerning the non-partiality factor, nearly all federal judges have their own individual political ideology which leans either to conservatism or liberalism. And while contemporary judges should ideally reflect total impartiality, in reality it is expected their judgments will reflect their ideology. That is a primary reason for their appointment.

Israel also had their version of a 'supreme court'.

"If cases come before your courts that are too difficult for you to judge – take them to the place the LORD your God will choose. Go to the priests....and to the judge who

is in office at that time. Inquire of them and they will give you the verdict. You must act according to the decisions they give you...Do not turn aside from what they tell you, to the right or to the left." Deuteronomy 17:8-11

The benchmark for justice at both levels of Israel's court system was God's immutable, absolute commandments. The benchmark for America today i.e. the constitution is open to interpretation of both act and intent according to the judge's ideology.

The issue of political correctness, a concept thousands of years old, also affects our judicial system.

"Yet at the same time many even among the leaders believed in him. But because of the Pharisees they would not confess their faith...for they loved praise from men more than praise from God." John 12:42-43

The concept of impartiality in our federal court system is laughable. In addition the benchmark for justice in this present generation has little to do with God's immutable laws.

Judicial Impartiality Begins with the President

One of the most significant privileges of the President is to appoint high level judges including Supreme Court justices. It's a sad commentary that most presidents will nominate judges who share ideologies similar to their own. George W. Bush during his presidency appointed John Roberts and Samuel Alito to the highest court.

Before being elected president, then Senator Obama was displeased with President Bush's choices saying they lacked the 'quality of empathy, of understanding and identifying with people's hopes and struggles.' In other words, President Bush's nominees wouldn't 'feel the pain' of common people.

The Bible has much to say about the qualifications of a judge and the manner in which judgment should be exercised.

When the Jews were preparing to enter the Promised Land, Moses addressed them regarding judging and administering the law. Because the Jews were so large in number Moses couldn't possibly hear every case himself. Therefore, judges were to be appointed to administer the law that God had set forth.

"The LORD your God has increased your numbers so that today you are as many as the stars in the sky...how can I bear your problems and your burdens and your disputes all by myself. Choose some wise, understanding and respected men from each of your tribes, and I will set them over you... And I charged your judges at that time: 'Hear the disputes between your brothers and judge fairly...Do not be afraid of any man, for judgment belongs to God.'" Deuteronomy 1:10, 12-13, 16-17

So while President Bush nominated judges that issued opinions that leaned to the conservative right when judging, such appointments were chastised by the then liberal Senator Obama.

Now President Obama has issued his own criteria for Supreme Court justices.

"We need somebody who's got the heart – the empathy – to recognize what it's like to be a teenage mom. The empathy to understand what it's like to be poor or African

American or gay or disabled or old – and that's the criteria by which I'll be selecting my judges."

Such criteria clearly violate the scriptural principle of impartiality in judging.

To attempt to 'balance' the Supreme Court with as many liberal leaning justices as there are conservative leaning justices defeats the entire concept of impartiality. This is another case where man thinks he has a better idea for administering justice and interpreting the law than God.

"Woe to those who are wise in their own eyes and clever in their own sight." Isaiah 5:21

Ideological Supreme Court Justices

The title phrase of this section has been in the headlines in recent years as the high court listened to arguments relative to the 'Affordable Health Care Act'. The title words are also the epitome of oxymora. It is accepted that 4 of the 9 Supreme Court justices lean to the left while 4 lean to the right leaving 1 to represent the 'middle of the road' or the 'swing' vote.

The Supreme Court is the final word whether an issue is in line with or at odds with the constitution of the United States. One of the Supreme Court justices, i.e. Ruth Bader Ginsburg, has recently voiced her opinion that the constitution is not presently adequate for modern progressivism. In addition, there are issues brought before the highest court that are totally anti-scriptural.

That brings to the foreground the question, does the Bible trump the constitution of the United States and the opinions of Supreme Court justices, or is the Bible irrelevant and outdated for today. Once again, each individual is free to have and express their opinion.

For those who believe the Bible is relevant, there are numerous Scripture references to reinforce their position. The Bible presents the argument that the ultimate benchmark for justice is the righteousness of God and the role of ultimate judge has been given to Christ.

"For he has set a day when he will judge the world with justice by the man he has appointed. He has given proof of this to all men by raising him from the dead." Acts 17:31

The Apostle John revealed that the future judgment of Christ will not be compromised, argued, or negotiated.

"I saw heaven standing open and there before me was a white horse, whose rider is called Faithful and True. With justice he judges and makes war." Revelation 19:11

Note that in both of the preceding passages Christ will judge the world and all its citizens in righteousness. Righteousness in the Greek means that which is just and right according to God and it covers much more than that contained in our constitution.

For example, while coveting and adultery are forbidden according to God's righteous laws, such activities are not forbidden by the constitution.

Further consider that even though an issue such as abortion is absolute according to God, Supreme Court justices will consider such an issue based on their individual ideological framework.

According to the Bible an issue is either right or wrong; it is either just or unjust. It either meets God's standard or it doesn't. There are no external circumstances that affect the issue, i.e. there is no partiality with God.

In summary, the Bible states that partiality in our court system will continue until the righteous Judge arrives and all wrongs will be made right.

And the benchmark for judgment will be the righteousness of God which no man on his own can attain.

III) Examining Partisan Politics

Partisan Politics is not new

There is a detailed example of partisan politics found in the Old Testament foreshadowing two contemporary but profoundly different political ideologies.

Recall that King Solomon in an attempt to please his many wives became involved in idolatry. That action brought severe consequences on himself and Israel.

"The LORD became angry with Solomon because his heart had turned away from the LORD, the God of Israel... So the LORD said to Solomon, 'Since this is your attitude and you have not kept my covenant and my decrees, which I commanded you, I will most certainly tear the kingdom away from you and give it to one of your subordinates.'" 1 Kings 11:9, 11

The Scripture provides great details about how God raised up adversaries to Solomon and then in more detail describes the debate between the two contenders for the kingship of Israel.

"Then the LORD raised up against Solomon an adversary...And God raised up against Solomon another

adversary...Also, Jeroboam son of Nebat rebelled against the king. He was one of Solomon's officials..." 1 Kings 11:14, 23, 26

The adversarial relationship was actually between Solomon's son Rehoboam, the presumed king by lineage, and Solomon's servant Jeroboam.

"So they sent for Jeroboam, and he and the whole assembly of Israel went to Rehoboam and said to him: 'Your father put a heavy yoke on us, but now lighten the harsh labor and the heavy yoke he put on us, and we will serve you.'" 1 Kings 12:3-4

In other words, Jeroboam suggested that Solomon's government required too much from the people and Rehoboam should lessen the burden imposed on the citizens.

Rehoboam listened to the proposal and told Jeroboam to give him three days to think about it. Rehoboam then consulted his advisors who also had much wisdom having served his father Solomon. They spoke from experience.

"They replied, 'If today you will be a servant to these people and serve them and give them a favorable answer, they will always be your servants.'" 1 Kings 12:7

Their advice was that the king should be a servant to the people and not that the people should be servants to the king.

"But Rehoboam rejected the advice the elders gave him and consulted the young men who had grown up with him and were serving him." 1 Kings 12:8

The 'expected to be' king rejected the wisdom of the elders and sought the advice of the current generation and their ideology.

The younger generation advised Rehoboam on how to respond to the suggestion that government should become less intrusive.

"*...tell them, 'My little finger is thicker than my father's waist. My father laid on you a heavy yoke; I will make it even heavier. My father scourged you with whips; I will scourge you with scorpions (scourges)'*" 1 Kings 12:10b-11

The Scripture states that Rehoboam responded arrogantly as he rejected their proposal to reduce governmental micro management of the citizenry.

"*So the king did not listen to the people, for this turn of events was from the LORD to fulfill the word the LORD had spoken...*" 1 Kings 12:15a

These events describe the division of national Israel into the northern ten tribes which would be referred to as Israel (and or Ephraim) and the southern tribes of Judah and Benjamin would be known as Judah. Jeroboam ruled over the northern tribes while Rehoboam ruled over the south.

God's sovereignty is nearly incomprehensible in detail. He executes His plan perfectly in whatever way He chooses.

Thus partisan politics has been active for thousands of years and will continue through this present age.

As Solomon said, *"There is nothing new under the sun."*

Partisan politics will, however, cease to be during the millennial kingdom and thereafter.

Liberalism or Conservatism: Which is more Biblical?

The answer to the title question is readily available; that is, if one gives credibility to Biblical teachings.

Firstly let's define both the political philosophies of liberalism and conservatism according to Webster.

Liberalism is a political philosophy based on belief in progress, the essential goodness of the human race… Liberalism subscribes to the premise that government should be the instrument to implement social justice. One will quickly note the similarities of liberalism and progressivism.

Conservatism, on the other hand, is a political philosophy based on tradition and social stability…the tendency to prefer an existing or traditional situation to change.

Contrary to liberalism, conservatism favors less government intervention in society and individual's affairs. Therefore, while progressivism is identified with liberalism, the Tea Party espouses the conservative political philosophy.

Now then, armed with definitions, it can be determined which political philosophy is closer to Biblical principles.

Initially the liberal premise relative to the 'essential goodness of the human race' can be addressed.

"Surely I was sinful at birth, sinful from the time my mother conceived me." Psalm 51:5

King David asserts in the above that all mankind, since Adam, is not born innately or essentially good but rather all mankind is born with a predisposition to sin.

Next, the liberal premise of progress implies change. In fact President Obama campaigned on the promise to deliver 'change we can believe in.' The Bible is very clear, however, that the basic rules of conduct given by God do not require change to keep pace with societal trends.

The benchmark by which all mankind is evaluated was revealed millennia ago and is immutable. The problem arises when man attempts to update God's instructions to fit the contemporary norm.

Such an attempt to update or reinterpret Biblical teachings brings disaster. Over and over again in the scriptures mankind is encouraged to return to the basics. The Hebrew for return is *shuv* and can be interpreted as repent, turn, and/or go back. *Shuv* can further be defined as a movement back to the point of departure, i.e. a reversal in direction.

"Perhaps when the people of Judah hear about every disaster I plan to inflict on them, each of them will turn from his wicked way; then I will forgive their wickedness and their sin." Jeremiah 36:3

"Ever since the time of your forefathers you have turned away from my decrees and have not kept them. Return to me, and I will return to you..." Malachi 3:7

Both of the above passages teach that to stray from God's ordinances will ultimately bring adversity and in both passages God invites man to return to the basics, i.e. the original ordinances of God in order to receive His blessings.

Perhaps the best known scripture passage containing the premise of turning back to God is:

"When I shut up the heavens so that there is no rain, or command locusts to devour the land or send a plague among my people, if my people, who are called by my name, will humble themselves and pray and seek my face and turn from their wicked ways, then will I hear from heaven and

will forgive their sin and will heal their land." 2 Chronicles 7:13-14

This passage vividly reaffirms that God controls the rain. Therefore, a drought is not a random occurrence, i.e. such adversity is in the hands of a sovereign God. Such adversity serves as 'wake-up calls'. In this light an adversity can be considered to be an 'olive branch' extended by a pleading God to get man's attention.

When there is no rain and the locusts devour the land there is famine. Famine and pestilence are not limited to the Old Testament.

For example, the result of the four horsemen of the future apocalypse described in the final book of the Bible can be summarized thusly:

"...They were given power over a fourth of the earth to kill by sword, famine and plague, and by the wild beasts of the earth." Revelation 6:8b

It appears that mankind in total will not 'return' or 'go back to the point of departure' but will continue to 'progress' towards contemporary norms which, according to the Bible, lead to destruction.

Is the Tea Party a Threat to Liberalism?

What is it about the Tea Party that liberalism finds so irksome? Of a surety the Tea Party leaves no question about what they stand for and what they don't.

Firstly, the Tea Party believes in smaller government and less taxes. The Tea Party believes the US government spends money on programs that are not Biblically based.

Recall the Scripture's definition of governmental leaders and their limited authority.

"For he is God's servant to do you good. But if you do wrong, be afraid, for he does not bear the sword for nothing... Therefore, it is necessary to submit to the authorities...This is also why you pay taxes..." Romans 13:4-6

The Tea Party believes very strongly that the government should operate within its means and not generate deficits which result in debt.

"Suppose one of you wants to build a tower, Will he not first sit down and estimate the cost to see if he has enough money to complete it? For if he lays the foundation and is not able to finish it, everyone who sees it will ridicule him, saying, 'This fellow began to build and was not able to finish.'" Luke 14:28-30

Thus far the Tea Party's fiscal philosophy appears to be Biblically based. How about their primary social issues?

The Tea Party opposes abortion.

"They turned their backs to me and not their faces; though I taught them again and again, they would not listen or respond to discipline...They built high places for Baal... to sacrifice their sons and daughters to Molech, though I never commanded, not did it enter my mind, that they should do such a detestable thing..." Jeremiah 32:33, 35

The Tea Party also supports traditional marriage between a man and a woman.

"For this reason a man will leave his father and mother and be united to his wife, and they will become one flesh." Genesis 2:24

'Wife' in this passage is from the Hebrew *Ishshah* which means female as opposed to a male. Jesus reaffirmed the above passage in the gospels as did Paul in the epistles.

Therefore, the major issues endorsed by the Tea Party appear to be Biblically based. Due to political pressures from both sides of the aisle, Tea Party members are being encouraged to compromise their ideals in order to enact legislation acceptable to both conservatives and liberals.

Recall the Biblical story where Samuel relayed God's instructions to Saul to totally destroy the Amalekites and all their animals. Well Saul, in an attempt to be a people pleaser, compromised God's instructions and while he did destroy the Amalekites, with the exception of their king Agag, he kept the animals which he said were for sacrifices to God. Samuel confronted Saul about his compromise and Saul realized his error.

"Then Saul said to Samuel, 'I have sinned. I violated the LORD's command and your instructions. I was afraid of the people and so I gave in to them.'" 1 Samuel 15:24

Partial obedience, i.e. compromise and political correctness cost Saul his kingship. The Tea Party today is also aware of the cost to compromise.

Does the Tea Party pose a real or perceived threat to liberalism? For sure, opposition to the Tea Party is definitely increasing as their ideology is made known. Self professed liberal congresswoman Maxine Waters while addressing members of the SEIU proclaimed boldly, "The Tea Party can go straight to hell…and I intend to help them get there."

Perhaps the economy is not the major challenge facing America today.

Compromise is good…Isn't it?

Senate majority leader Harry Reid is really fed up with the newer and younger republicans in congress (those pesky tea partiers). After one of the recent impasses Reid stated he hopes those new members have learned their lesson, i.e. they must learn to compromise.

That sounds logical and practical as a necessary part of democracy, however, according to the Bible democracy will fail in the future after running its course.

Therefore, if certain representatives stand their ground on political issues which are backed by scriptural teachings, are they to be demeaned for not compromising?

Recall that King Saul lost his kingship because he compromised God's instructions.

The prophet Samuel responded:

"…You have rejected the word of the LORD, and the LORD has rejected you as king over Israel!" 1 Samuel 15:26b

In the case of freshmen representatives, compromising meant not only to agree to anti-scriptural legislation but also to break their promise to their constituents.

Man's logical thinking that the end justifies the means is not scriptural. God's realm is perfection and nothing less can satisfy a Holy and just God. Inasmuch as man is created in God's image, perfection is also required of man.

"Be perfect, therefore, as your heavenly Father is perfect." Matthew 5:48

Perfect in the scriptures has several synonyms including sinless and completed for the purpose intended. The Bible states that all have sinned, therefore, the need for a perfect sinless substitute, i.e. Christ.

Now if our ultimate future depends solely on the merits and perfection of Christ, what would have been the consequences if He had given in to compromise? That's exactly what Satan tried to accomplish.

At the beginning of Christ's earthly ministry Satan tempted Him to avoid the cross.

"The devil led him up to a high place and showed him in an instant all the kingdoms of the world. And he said to him, 'I will give you all their authority and splendor, for it has been given to me, and I can give it to anyone I want to. So if you worship me, it will all be yours.'" Luke 4:5-7

Satan knew all the kingdoms of the world would be given to Christ anyway. He offered Christ the reward without having to pay the price. Christ would not compromise God's word.

Then near the end of Christ's earthly ministry in the Garden of Gethsemane there arose again the issue of paying the price.

"Going a little farther, he fell to the ground and prayed that if possible the hour might pass from him. 'Abba, Father,' he said, 'everything is possible for you. Take this cup from me. Yet not what I will, but what you will.'" Mark 14:35-36

And again we saw that Christ would not compromise. Imagine the consequences for us if He had.

And then in the early church there is a great example of taking a stand for the truth and rejecting the easy way out. Peter and John were told not to speak nor teach in the name of Jesus. Their response was quick and decisive.

"But Peter and John replied, 'Judge for yourselves whether it is right in God's sight to obey you rather than God. For we cannot help speaking about what we have seen and heard.'" Acts 4:19-20

Compromise is but another form of age old hypocrisy called political correctness.

There will be those who think Biblical principles have no place in government. This is America and everyone is free to have and express their opinion. In the mean-time, however, should those who will not compromise Biblical principles in all aspects of life be ostracized for their stand?

Division is a Sign of the Times

Many objective observers note that this nation is presently extremely polarized relative to political ideologies. But does the division have a deeper meaning? There are those who believe that political ideology should be kept separate from religion while others believe that the Bible can help explain contemporary political issues.

And then there are those who believe that Jesus would be the answer to all division and would bring peace to the whole world when He was born.

"For to us a child is born, to us a son is given...Of the increase of his government and peace there will be no end. He will reign on David's throne and over his kingdom, establishing and upholding it with justice and righteousness from that time on and forever." Isaiah 9:6-7

The wording 'from that time on' reveals that peace would follow judgment and will be fulfilled when Christ returns to earth and begins His rule during the millennial kingdom. But the purpose of His birth and mission during His initial advent was substantially different.

"I have come to bring fire on the earth, and how I wish it were already kindled! But I have a baptism to undergo, and how distressed I am until it is completed! Do you think I came to bring peace on earth? No, I tell you, but division." Luke 12:49-51

Inasmuch as history is presently between Christ's first advent and His return, the earth should expect division which is proactively initiated and given by Christ Himself. He speaks of His impending sacrificial death to redeem mankind which must first take place before He can bring peace on the earth. He wishes that the time of His return to judge the earth was already here.

The division He speaks of is the division between those who accept His deity and gift of redemption versus those who choose to go it on their own. According to the Bible any other divisions among men are totally subsidiary to the ultimate division.

There are, however, correlations between differing political ideologies and the ultimate division among men. There are many who believe that political factions should be willing to compromise in order to solve national problems.

Even some 'church' spokesmen believe there should be unity among factions. Such tactics are not scripturally based.

God's standard of justice and righteousness are absolute and not subject to compromise. The common and popular premise that 'we should all get along' for the good of the nation is perhaps well intended but not backed by Scripture.

Christians are admonished to take a stand for Biblical principles and not waiver. Jesus also taught that taking a stand would cause division and hatred.

"All men will hate you because of me..." Matthew 10:22a

"Then you will be handed over to be persecuted and put to death, and you will be hated by all nations because of me." Matthew 24:9

Jesus also gave a warning to those who would cave and deny Him.

"But whoever disowns me before men, I will disown him before my Father in heaven." Matthew 10:33

Therefore, division is present and should be recognized as well as expected. It is a sign of the times.

"...When you see a cloud rising in the west, immediately you say, 'It's going to rain,' and it does. And when the south wind blows, you say, 'It's going to be hot,' and it is. Hypocrites! You know how to interpret the appearance of the earth and the sky. How is it that you don't know how to interpret this present time?" Luke 12:54-56

Thus there will be those who miss the 'big picture' and focus on remedying political division while others will smile and say to themselves, 'God's plan is right on schedule.'

Progressivism and the Bible

Anyone who has been exposed to the media recently has probably heard or seen the term 'progressive' used in the context of political affiliation or ideology. In the political and social context progressivism is associated with change or reform. It re-emerged as a very popular concept in the late 19th and early 20th century as a means to improve the social environment to keep pace with technological changes being experienced in industry and large corporations.

The basic concept of progressivism, however, has roots dating back to the Renaissance. Contrary to widely held Christian beliefs that mankind was struggling and was destined for a transitory journey on earth ending in judgment, philosophers advanced the idea that there was no reason that mankind shouldn't enjoy a better quality of life here and now.

Later thinking even referenced Darwin's thoughts on biological evolution to justify social improvement. "And as natural selection works solely by and for the good of each being, all corporeal and mental environments will tend to progress towards perfection." That school of thought fostered the idea that continual social progress would result in social perfection.

The subsequent implication was the world was becoming a better place, a thought found nowhere in the Bible. If that were true there would be no book of Revelation.

Progressivism at the time of the industrial revolution in the United States embraced and pursued the idea of social justice for all. Proponents believed government should level the playing field for everyone. As such, progressives today typically support organized labor and trade unions, believe in and promote a minimum wage, and would support such issues as a universal health care system. This ideology promotes the redistribution of wealth via a progressive income tax system.

As previously noted, progressivism is typically more closely associated with liberalism than conservatism.

When campaigning for president for his first term the major campaign issue for Barack Obama was 'fundamental change' of how America functions. The typical campaign message for conservative candidates on the other hand is to get back to the basics and return to the principles on which this nation was founded.

In the Bible God outlined His plan for mankind and described in great detail how man was to act towards his Creator, towards one another individually and toward others corporately.

The Bible also states clearly that God will hold all men accountable for how they receive and obey His instructions. The benchmark for the future accounting is still the Bible. The benchmark hasn't changed; therefore, according to the Bible God will have no tolerance for those who have 'reformed' His instructions in the name of progress to accommodate contemporary special interests where such changes violate His original instructions.

"Do not add to what I command you and do not subtract from it, but keep the commands of the LORD your God that I give you." Deuteronomy 4:2

"Do not add to his words, or he will rebuke you and prove you a liar." Proverbs 30:6

And finally at the very end of the Bible are the words that summarize the fate of those who would add to or delete from God's word. Jesus, the Judge states:

"I warn everyone who hears the words of the prophecy of this book: If anyone adds anything to them, God will add

to him the plagues described in this book. And if anyone takes words away from this book of prophecy, God will take away from him his share in the tree of life and in the holy city, which are described in this book." Revelation 22:18-19

Therefore, will those who attempt to legislate 'progress' by compromising God's laws to meet the desires of the current generation prosper, or will those who strive to return to the basics fare better.

IV) Presidential Politics and Scripture

Presidential Priorities

King Solomon, the wisest man in the world, and President Obama have one very significant thing in common, i.e. both were established in their office by God.

King Solomon acknowledged that premise:

"Now, O LORD my God, you have made your servant king in place of my father David. But I am only a little child and do not know how to carry out my duties." 1 Kings 3:7

And the Apostle Paul affirmed that truth in the New Testament, hence President Obama.

"Everyone must submit himself to the governing authorities, for there is no authority except that which God has established. The authorities that exist have been established by God." Romans 13:1

That is where the commonality stops.

In 2012 the United States was once again involved in election year politics. President Obama wanted to retain his position while Mitt Romney wanted to unseat him. And while both were trying to convince the electorate they were the best choice, as we've just seen, the final decision was God's.

And incidentally, the decision was made long before the campaigning began. That fact, however, shouldn't lessen our interest in voicing our opinion or exercising our right to vote inasmuch as God's providence and man's choice are totally compatible.

Perhaps the issue that most differentiated the two presidential candidates was who was best able to improve the status of all citizens, i.e. the government, or the citizens themselves. Those who believe the government is best able to improve each individual's lot must also realize that government doesn't generate revenue.

Government must take revenue from individual citizens or corporations that have, and redistribute it to those who have not. In fact that was one of President Obama's primary campaign issues. Romney contended that individuals in the private sector should be able to keep more of their earnings and have unfettered opportunity to pursue the American dream on their own.

Who is right? Much insight can be gleaned from the Bible. What did King Solomon do?

Shortly after Solomon began his rule as king, God asked him what he desired to have. Solomon without hesitation replied.

"...You have shown great kindness to your servant, my father David, because he was faithful to you and righteous and upright in heart. You have continued this great kindness to him and have given him a son to sit on his throne this very day." 1 Kings 3:6

Before making his request to God, Solomon acknowledged that his father, David, had found favor with God because he lived and exercised his kingship in the light of God's righteousness and truth. Solomon was now placed in the position to continue his father's legacy.

"Your servant is here among the people you have chosen, a great people, too numerous to count or number. So give your servant a discerning heart to govern your people and to distinguish between right and wrong..." 1 Kings 3:8-9

Solomon confessed that on his own he was totally inadequate to do his job. He, therefore, asked God to grant him wisdom to be able to discern between good and evil so he could judge God's people properly. He further stated that no man on his own was capable of judging correctly.

"The LORD was pleased that Solomon had asked for this. So God said to him, 'Since you have asked for this and not for long life or wealth for yourself...but for discernment in administering justice, I will do what you have asked. I will give you a wise and discerning heart...Moreover, I will give you what you have not asked for – both riches and honor – and if you walk in my ways and obey my statutes and commands as David your father did, I will give you a long life.'" 1 Kings 3:10-14

Notice the continued emphasis on obedience to God's statutes and commandments.

During the 2012 campaign President Obama was looking for a new campaign slogan. A Good suggestion would have been:

"Are we closer to God's standard of justice today than we were four years ago?"

Subtle Defiance

One of the major tenets of the Bible is that all mankind are assigned to just two groups; those with saving faith in God and those without which translates once again to those preserved for everlasting life or those reserved for everlasting darkness.

Those with saving faith give the highest priority in their lives to spiritual matters while those without do not. The latter may appear to live an exemplary lifestyle but their major priority might be to exact all they can from this lifetime. The Bible has much to say about those whose priorities focus on the present instead of the future.

Recently both presidential candidates, especially Governor Romney, stated repeatedly that every individual should have the right to pursue and achieve the 'American Dream'. The incumbent president on the other hand didn't focus on that issue; his ideology included the concept that government should provide all that one might dream of having.

The concept of governmental provision can be discarded immediately as unscriptural, but is the American dream in line with Biblical teachings? One popular definition of the dream is as follows:

"The American Dream is…a set of ideals in which freedom includes the opportunity for prosperity, success, and an upward social mobility achievable through hard work."

According to this definition the attainment of the American dream can be measured in material terms and upward social mobility, both of which are said to be achievable through personal effort.

Let it be reiterated at this point that material success and upward social mobility are not in themselves 'evil' or necessarily to be classified as sin. The issue centers on one's priorities, or where one places their trust.

Jesus addressed the issues contained in the American dream succinctly.

"So do not worry, saying, 'What shall we eat?' or 'What shall we drink?' or 'What shall we wear?' For the pagans run after all these things, and your heavenly Father knows that you need them. But seek first his kingdom and his righteousness, and all these things will be given to you as well. Therefore do not worry about tomorrow..." Matthew 6:31-34a

Jesus was explaining the difference between needs and wants and then He plainly stated that one's top priority should be to seek the righteousness of God. If one's priorities were in order, then they needn't worry about their needs being met.

Jesus taught his disciples in another passage, in which He was defining the cost of discipleship, that misplaced priorities could mean total failure.

"If anyone would come after me, he must deny himself and take up his cross and follow me. For whoever wants to save his life will lose it, but whoever loses his life for me will find it. What good will it be for a man if he gains the whole world, yet forfeits his soul? Or what can a man give in exchange for his soul?" Matthew 16:24-26

And while upward social mobility is also a significant aspect of the American dream, Jesus offered quite a different viewpoint. He was explaining both to the multitudes and His disciples that the scribes and Pharisees sought after and enjoyed social prominence.

"Everything they do is done for men to see...they love to be greeted in the marketplaces and to have men call them 'Rabbi.'" Matthew 23:5a, 7

Jesus went on to explain the ineffectiveness of the Pharisee's actions.

"The greatest among you will be your servant. For whoever exalts himself will be humbled, and whoever humbles himself will be exalted." Matthew 23:11-12

Thus it is apparent that the messages from both presidential candidates fell far short of scriptural teachings. But then, how many votes would a candidate have received if he had campaigned on scriptural issues?

Hopefully this great nation will find itself and the issues in 2016 will be substantially different.

And while priorities may not appear on the surface to play a significant role in defining a person's spiritual condition, in reality the opposite is true. An individual's priorities are in fact a subtle indicator of which of the two basic groups of mankind one belongs.

A Parable for the President

During a National Day of Prayer observance President Obama made reference to the inequality of wealth among Americans.

America's Vision vs. God's Standard of Justice

He suggested that the solution was to redistribute wealth, or simply take money from the 'haves' and give it to the 'have-nots'.

From his own words:

"And when I talk about shared responsibility, it's because I genuinely believe that in a time when many folks are struggling, at a time when we have enormous deficits, it's hard for me to ask seniors on a fixed income, or young people with student loans, or middle-class families who can barely pay the bills to shoulder the burden alone. And I think to myself, if I'm willing to give something up as somebody who's been extraordinarily blessed, and give up some of the tax breaks that I enjoy, I actually think that's going to make economic sense."

Then he added, "But for me as a Christian, it also coincides with Jesus' teaching that *'...For unto whom much is given, much shall be required.'*" Luke 12:48b

Even though he may have meant well, his speech writers should have alerted him that his fiscal ideology doesn't coincide with Jesus' teaching quoted, i.e. the Parable of the Faithful Steward has nothing to do with money.

The key to understanding the intended meaning of the passage he quoted is to examine the very first word, i.e. 'for'.

The Greek base defining 'for' is a causative particle following a statement and expresses and/or affirms and explains what has just been stated.

Now let's examine the specific parable which the President quoted in order to get the actual context.

"That servant who knows his master's will and does not get ready or does not do what his master wants will be beaten with many blows. But the one who does not know and does things deserving punishment will be beaten with few blows. For (from) everyone who has been given much, much will be demanded..." Luke 12:47-48

Jesus was explaining that once a steward knew of his master's will but purposely disregarded it during his master's absence, that steward would be punished severely upon his master's return.

But if a servant/steward did things deserving of punishment without realizing his error, i.e. not knowing his master's will, his punishment would be less severe.

The 'much is given' in the teaching is the extent of the master's will that had been known by and entrusted to the steward. The 'much will be required' is the stewardship of the knowledge of his master's will.

There is, however, a great parable in Matthew's gospel that does relate stewardship of the knowledge of spiritual things with the redistribution of wealth. In fact the wording states that the stewardship of such knowledge is like the stewardship of money. The parable is known as the Parable of the Talents.

"Again, it will be like a man going on a journey, who called his servants and entrusted his property to them. To one he gave five talents of money, to another two talents, and to another one talent, each according to his ability. Then he went on his journey." Matthew 25:14-15

The Greek base for 'like' means a comparison, more specifically described as 'just as', 'wholly as', or 'exactly as'.

A 'talent' is a unit of measure. In this parable a talent refers to a significant amount of money. The parable describes how servants, entrusted with differing amounts of their masters assets, use and grow such assets during his absence, or during the present 'church' age. The parable ends with the master's return and the required accounting of the assets entrusted to each servant.

"The man who had received the five talents went at once and put his money to work and gained five more. So also, the one with the two talents gained two more. But the man who had received the one talent went off, dug a hole in the ground and hid his master's money. After a long time the master of those servants returned and settled accounts with them." Matthew 25:16-19

The first two servants, although originally given different amounts of the master's assets, both exercised faithful stewardship and doubled that which was entrusted to them.

The master's response to both of them:

"His master replied, 'Well done, good and faithful servant(s)! You have been faithful with a few things; I will put you in charge of many things...'" Matthew 25:21

Now the third servant did not invest the assets entrusted to him, in fact he hid those assets. In financial terms, he took them out of circulation. He attempted to justify his actions by even questioning his master's motives.

Upon the master's return he confronted that servant about his slothfulness. The master told his servant that even if he questioned his motives and didn't want to take a risk, he should have entrusted the assets to his banker and at least earn interest.

"Well then, you should have put my money on deposit with the bankers, so that when I returned I would have received it back with interest." Matthew 25:27

The major thrust of this parable is that spiritual insights given by Jesus to His servants must be circulated in order to grow in the same manner as capital productivity.

Jesus went on to say:

"Take the talent from him (the slothful servant) and give it to the one who has the ten talents." Matthew 25:28

Perhaps President Obama who likes to justify his political agenda with scripture will rethink his redistribution position by borrowing the following quote from Jesus.

"For everyone who has will be given more, and he will have an abundance. Whoever does not have, even what he has will be taken from him." Matthew 25:29

It appears that Jesus' definition of redistribution is exactly opposite to that espoused by President Obama.

Parables were, however, a significant part of Jesus' teaching and were used to illustrate and explain the kingdom of heaven.

Matthew records an example of Jesus presenting a parable and then provides an answer as to why He used parables in His teaching.

"Then he told them many things in parables..." Matthew 13:3a

"The disciples came to him and asked, 'Why do you speak to the people in parables?' He replied, 'The knowledge of the secrets of the kingdom of heaven has been given to you,

but not to them...This is why I speak to them in parables... In them is fulfilled the prophecy of Isaiah: You will be ever hearing but never understanding; you will be ever seeing but never perceiving; For this people's heart has become calloused...'" Matthew 13:10-11, 13-15a

Notice the last sentence in the above; it begins with 'for' which explains the preceding thoughts.

Thus according to Jesus, His disciples would understand and be enlightened by His parables but those who were not His disciples would not understand them.

Another Parable Invoked by the President

During one of his major speeches on the economy President Obama cited a popular Biblical passage to compare his strategic plans, i.e. stimulus, to revive America's sagging economy. He stated in part:

"Now there's a parable at the end of the sermon on the mount that tells the story of two men. The first built his house on a pile of sand, and it was soon destroyed when a storm hit. But the second is known as the wise man, for when 'the rain descended, and the floods came, and the winds blew, and beat upon the house, it fell not: for it was founded on a rock.'"

"That's the new foundation we must build. That's our house built upon a rock. That must be our future…and my administration's policies are designed to achieve that future. That is the house upon the rock…proud, sturdy, unwavering in the face of the greatest storms…I have no doubt that this house will stand and the dream of our founders will live on in our time."

No doubt millions of Americans were encouraged to hear the president compare his policies with scriptural teachings. The parable that he cited is very popular indeed. Let's review the original parable and compare it with Mr. Obama's words and his assessment of that parable.

Actually Mr. Obama's rendition picks up right after the situational setting of the parable. Now this is very significant because Jesus puts the parable of the two men and their houses within a specific context.

*"Therefore everyone who hears these words of mine **and puts them into practice** is like a wise man who built his house on the rock. The rain came down, the streams rose, and the winds blew and beat against that house; yet it did not fall, because it had its foundation on the rock. But everyone who hears these words of mine **and does not put them into practice** is like a foolish man who built his house on sand. The rain came down, the streams rose and the winds blew and beat against that house, and it fell with a great crash."* Matthew 7:24-27 (emphasis added)

The parable very clearly states that the wise man who built his house on the rock applies to the man who hears Jesus' teachings and does them. The foolish man who builds his house on the sand is one who hears those same teachings but rejects them. That is the specific context for the parable.

Consider for example that on his first day as president Mr. Obama announced that he would issue an executive order to reinstate funding internationally for groups that perform or promote abortions.

Consider further: does his position of redistribution of wealth via taxation coincide with Biblical principles? How about mass government sponsored entitlement programs?

How about his strategy for peace in the Middle East? How about his tolerance of those who are attempting to overthrow this country and install a religion not taught in the Bible?

How about his tolerance of those who are overtly removing God from daily life, i.e. removing 'In God We Trust' from the new dollar coin or removing 'Under God' from the pledge of allegiance? How about legislation that tolerates anti-biblical teachings because they have become the societal norm?

How about the appointment of judges having ideologies that conflict with biblical teachings?

Everyone has the freedom to examine the facts and decide for themselves whether political rhetoric is substance or fluff. We should be particularly observant to see if those who claim Christianity and cite the Bible really understand it, and furthermore are prepared to live up to what they say.

The Silent Mockery

Throughout the history of Judaism and Christianity there have been those who have exercised their freedom to mock the word of God. Mocking has several forms, i.e. from actually scoffing at Old Testament prophecies to just not taking the Bible seriously.

In the Old Testament writings the same Hebrew word is used interchangeably for mock and scoff. Synonyms for mock and scoff in both testaments include scorn and ridicule.

In the Old Testament the greatest offenders were God's chosen people themselves, the Israelites.

"The LORD, the God of their fathers, sent word to them through his messengers again and again because he had pity on his people...But they mocked God's messengers, despised his words and scoffed at his prophets until the wrath of the LORD was aroused against his people and there was no remedy." 2 Chronicles 36:15-16

The current prevailing form of mockery is to claim to be a Christian but then not take God's word seriously. This is also a form of hypocrisy but it is so prevalent in America today that it is hardly recognized as such.

For example, only three of the original Ten Commandments are considered laws in our present judicial system. That means that we can break six (excluding the Sabbath) of the original commandments with no legal recourse. Do we think that those remaining six are not as important to the author of those original ten as the three that we have adopted into our legal system?

The truth is that not taking those other commandments seriously is a primary cause of this country's present problems. For example ask nearly any politician what they consider to be this nation's number one problem and the answer will most likely be the status of our economy. We are considered to be the leader of the free world not only because of our military strength but also because of our financial strength and the size of our economy.

Remember within a week of 9-11 former President Bush said that America would show the world how powerful and resilient we were by how quickly the stock market would be up and running. It was as if we were ignoring commandment number one.

"I am the LORD your God, who brought you out of Egypt, out of the land of slavery. You shall have no other gods before me." Exodus 20:2-3

The Obama administration is not faring any better with the issue of not taking the Bible seriously than the previous administration. President Obama believes that we can negotiate with Iran, the country whose leader wants to annihilate Israel.

President Obama also believes that the solution to the Palestinian issue is to allow them sovereign nation status within Israel's existing borders. In addition this administration thinks that the way to solve this country's economic woes is to add more debt. Such strategies are all counter-Biblical.

America and the rest of the world appear to be perfectly content to continue with this silent mockery of the word of God as if things will continue indefinitely as they are.

"Dear friends...I want you to recall the words spoken in the past by the holy prophets...First of all, you must understand that in the last days scoffers will come...They will say, 'Where is this 'coming' he promised? Ever since our fathers died, everything goes on as it has since the beginning of creation.' But they deliberately forget that long ago by God's word ...the world of that time was deluged and destroyed. By the same word the present heavens and earth

are reserved for fire, being kept for the day of judgment and destruction..." 2 Peter 3:1-7

It appears that we have forgotten the history of the flood which was caused by ignoring God's authority.

The advantages of avoiding mockery, scoffing, and scorning God's word is addressed by King David in the very first Psalm.

"Blessed is the man who does not walk in the counsel of the wicked or stand in the way of sinners or sit in the seat of mockers. But his delight is in the law of the LORD..." Psalm 1:1-2a

V) President Obama's Position on Islam

Excerpts from the President's Speech Directed to the Muslim World

Some of the final quotes from President Obama's Cairo speech to the Muslim world include, "We have the power to make the world we seek…The people of the world can live together in peace. We know this is God's vision."

President Obama seems to think that a consensus of nations can plot their own future. He overlooks the fact that according to his Bible the final alignment of the nations has already been established by the sovereign God of Abraham, Isaac, and Jacob.

When men think that the alignment of nations is at its strongest, it will really be at its weakest. Man's final attempt to align the nations into a one-world sovereignty was described by the prophet Daniel over 2,500 years ago. The history of the rise and fall of the nations was revealed in

King Nebuchadnezzar's dream interpreted and confirmed by Daniel.

The contents of Nebuchadnezzar's dream will be addressed in detail in chapter 6.

Nebuchadnezzar then had a second dream and Daniel also summarized its meaning.

"This is the interpretation, O king, and this is the decree the Most High has issued...the Most High is sovereign over the kingdoms of men and gives them to anyone he wishes." Daniel 4:24-25

In view of the above proclamation, President Obama had the audacity to say that man has 'the power to make the world we seek.' The president then addressed the noble goal of the entire world living together in peace.

"Jesus answered: 'Watch out that no one deceives you... You will hear of wars and rumors of wars...Nation will rise against nation, and kingdom against kingdom...All these are the beginning of birth pains." Matthew 24:4, 6-7

Throughout the Old Testament false prophets proclaimed peace for Israel.

"But I (Jeremiah) said, 'Ah, Sovereign LORD, the prophets keep telling them, you will not see the sword... Indeed, I will give you lasting peace in this place.' Then the LORD said to me, 'The prophets are prophesying lies in my name. I have not sent them or appointed them or spoken to them. They are prophesying to you false visions...and the delusions of their own minds.'" Jeremiah 14:13-14

While peace is an admirable goal it will not come about as suggested by president Obama. Peace will only come after man has made many futile attempts to achieve it on their own. According to President Obama's own Bible peace will only be realized after Christ returns to judge the kings of the earth and then He Himself will align and rule the nations.

"The Lord is at your right hand; he will crush kings on the day of his wrath. He will judge the nations...and crushing the rulers of the whole earth." Psalm 110:5-6

"He will rule them with an iron scepter; he will dash them to pieces like pottery..." Revelation 2:27

Therefore, the president's words, "the people of the world can live together in peace...we know this is God's vision" are really just his own vision and his naïve assessment of reality.

Inasmuch as Mr. Obama is our president, we should give him the benefit of the doubt and trust that he really thinks that he is saying and doing the right things. However, he is really speaking in total contradiction to his own Bible. But his words have great appeal to the politically correct and the Islamic community.

For Example Mr. Obama stated in his Cairo speech: "That is why I am committed to working with American Muslims to ensure that they can fulfill 'Zakat'. Zakat is defined as obligatory charitable giving by Muslims which is one of the 'Five Pillars of Islam'. Mr. Obama's pledge to help in this area will most likely be found in revisions to our tax code.

This section is in no way intended to be anti-Obama but rather to expose the inconsistencies of his Cairo speech where he claims that his vision and strategy is the same

"The United States allows Islamists to operate freely within the legal system. There is no need for them to break or to contradict our laws to achieve their takeover goals."

"The law is the most potent weapon used by Islamists. CAIR (Council on American-Islamic Relations) is an Islamic organization that retains a massive team of lawyers. They sue anybody who dares to say something that can be construed as objectionable about Islam."

"...since they (Islamists) don't have the military might that they once did...They've found a loophole that will work in their favor. It's our democratic laws that ensure freedom of speech, religious tolerance and equal rights for aliens as well as American citizens."

"America is a haven for followers of all beliefs. Ironically, those whom it strives to protect often attack America."

"Strangely, we tolerate those who despise and oppose the traditional spiritual values that most Americans embrace."

"I am not suggesting here that America abandons its virtues or even revise them. However, I do hope to draw attention to America's pressing need. We need to develop mechanisms that will close the loopholes that our enemies are using to gain dominance in our country. They are penetrating our defenses and damaging the foundations of our culture by deviously applying the virtues that made this country great."

"American values are like a ladder, Islamists use it to enter and conquer the American fortress. After reaching their goal, they will kick the ladder away."

"Be on your guard; stand firm in the faith; be men of courage; be strong." 1 Corinthians 16:13

Why the Renewed Interest in Islam?

One of the major reason for the renewed interest in Islam is the ongoing attempts by the State Department and Islamic leaders to reword and refine UN resolution 16/18 regarding free speech and defamation of religion. At this point it appears that America's freedom of speech may be threatened.

The Bible is very clear that everyone has the freedom of choice to either accept or reject the Christian message upon hearing it.

"If anyone will not welcome you or listen to your words, shake the dust off your feet when you leave that home or town." Matthew 10:14

This passage states if the message of the gospel of Jesus Christ is rejected the disciples were to move on and not retaliate. Rejection of the message will be settled at the end of the age, not by the disciples at the time of rejection. This premise is reinforced by the constitution of the United States.

"…prohibits the making of any law respecting an establishment of religion, impeding the free exercise of religion…"

Islam is likewise very zealous about their religion; however, rejection of the religion of Islam is a bit more serious.

Just as Islamic nations will not compromise their religion or their political ideology, i.e. sharia law, America should follow Islam's example and take a stand for her Christian foundation and constitution.

In a republic such as ours, ideological differences are settled by voter participation. For example, democrats and republicans have significant and seemingly irreconcilable differences; however, they may live next to each other, befriend each other, and even attend the same church together, but they will resolve their ideological differences at the ballot box.

"If it is possible, as far as it depends on you, live at peace with everyone. Do not take revenge, my friends, but leave room for God's wrath, for it is written: 'It is mine to avenge; I will repay,' says the Lord." Romans 12:18-19

The Islamic community and America agree, and it must be acknowledged with open dialogue that America's Christian foundation and constitution are incompatible with the religion of Islam and sharia law. And while Islam recognizes and openly declares that truth, America isn't giving them their due credibility. America needs to take them at their word.

The day is quickly approaching when the litmus test for a political candidate will not be whether the candidate is pro-life or pro-choice, but rather that candidate's position on giving away freedoms by accommodating ideologies contrary to America and all she stands for.

Multiculturalism is not the answer to such a challenge. In recent months German Chancellor Angela Merkel, British Prime Minister David Cameron, and departing French President Nicolas Sarkozy have all issued similar assessments describing the failures of the multicultural experience in Europe.

If America desires to remain a great nation, she must take a stand to protect her constitution, and the church must likewise take a stand to preserve her basic tenets which center on Christ.

Any influence or ideology which attempts to destroy America's hard fought freedoms or distort Christianity should be met with zealous opposition. Each small concession aimed at accommodating those opposed to America's way of life replaces one small freedom that was bought with blood.

Political correctness must go.

Many are beginning to ask, 'Why are these issues not being discussed in current debates, especially by those who claim to be conservatives?'

"...Strengthening Democracy..."

The drafters of United Nations resolution 16/18 repeatedly touted the benefits of open dialog addressing interfaith and intercultural issues at all levels as a means to 'strengthen democracy'. Perhaps the implementation of this resolution will encourage our government to rise above the destructive practice of political correctness and be serious about promoting open dialog about real issues.

One of the most critical issues, if not the most critical issue, facing the world today is the future of Israel. And while some may consider the Israeli issue to be primarily political in nature, the two largest religions in the world consider it to have basic religious roots. Biblical references unabashedly tell of Israel's glorious future while Islamic references speak of Israel's demise.

It is a simple truth that the Israeli issue is irreconcilable between Islamic nations, Christian nations, and the Jewish nation Israel itself. Therefore, the issue should be put on the table via open dialog so everyone is aware of the dilemma.

There is no question that Islam is doing a much better job of speaking openly about the Israeli challenge than is the United States. One of the most outspoken Muslim spokesmen was Iran's president Mahmoud Ahmedinejad. Ahmedinejad, a Shiite Muslim exercised his freedom of speech at the United Nations as well as such institutions as Columbia University. Ahmedinejad spoke out about Islam's twelfth Imam, or Mahdi (savior) who it is said will establish Islamic rule over the world. Ahmedinejad believes that he has been appointed to usher in their Mahdi. He has also voiced his support of Hamas' leadership in Gaza until the destruction of Israel.

Several of Ahmedinejad's many statements relative to Israel include:

- "The Islamic umma (community) will not allow its historic enemy (Israel) to live in its heartland."
- "Our dear Imam (Ayatollah Khomeini) ordered that the occupying regime in Jerusalem be wiped off the face of the earth...The issue of Palestine is not one which we could compromise on..."
- "The Zionist regime is counterfeit and illegitimate and cannot survive...The big powers have created this fraud regime..."

The Bible, on the other hand, presents an entirely different account of Israel and their future.

"For you are a people holy to the LORD your God. The LORD your God has chosen you out of all the peoples on the face of the earth to be his people, his treasured possession." Deuteronomy 7:6

"Then the nations will know that I the LORD make Israel holy, when my sanctuary is among them forever." Ezekiel 37:28

The above Old Testament passages are reaffirmed in the New Testament.

"I ask then: Did God reject his people? By no means! ...God did not reject his people, whom he foreknew." Romans 11:1-2

The Bible also gives a vivid account of Jerusalem's future.

"On that day the LORD will shield those who live in Jerusalem...On that day I will set out to destroy all the nations that attack Jerusalem." Zechariah 12:8-9

America's foreign policy should reflect the contributions from both Islamic literature and the Bible.

America's Strategic Challenge: Immigration or Emigration

For decades this great nation has been wrestling ineffectively with the issue of immigration and its affect on cultural and fiscal issues. However, considering recent legal challenges to the constitutionality of SQ 755 in Oklahoma perhaps the focus should shift to emigration.

Seventy percent of Oklahoma voters voted in favor of banning Oklahoma courts from considering international or Islamic law in their judicial system. It has been estimated that the percentage would have been well in excess of 90% if voters had a better understanding of sharia law.

The legality of SQ 755 was challenged by Muneer Awad, former executive director of the Council on American-Islamic Relations of Oklahoma, i.e. C.A.I.R.

In an Associated Press article Mr. Awad stated, "This is an important reminder that the Constitution is the last line of defense against a rising tide of anti-Muslim bigotry in our society...We are also hopeful that this decision serves as a reminder to politicians wishing to score political points through fear-mongering and bigotry."

An objective observer would not find any bigotry involved, rather the SQ 755 amendment is a pro-active move to preserve and protect both America's freedoms and Christian values. As far as the 'rising tide' noted by Mr. Awad, the real rising tide is a great awakening of America to the intrusion of an ideology openly declared by Islam to be incompatible with the American way of life and Christianity.

Americans are not anti-Muslim but rather very much pro-American and pro-Christian. It is refreshing to see that Americans all across the land are beginning to open their eyes and take note of compromising issues that are affecting not only this generation but following generations. People are starting to put it all together and realize this nation's freedoms are at risk.

The AP article further stated, "Awad argued that the ban on Islamic law would likely affect every aspect of his life as well as the execution of his will after his death." Americans do not wish any hardship for Mr. Awad.

On the contrary Americans desire Mr. Awad to realize his full potential; however, if his livelihood is contingent on sharia law, then the logical solution is for Mr. Awad to emigrate to a land where sharia is the prevailing legal system.

America provides Mr. Awad the freedom to practice his religion, but America is under no obligation to alter its legal system to accommodate Mr. Awad's specific needs.

Actually the treatment of non Muslims in Islamic nations is more scriptural than America's treatment of Muslims in America.

"The same law applies to the native-born and to the alien living among you." Exodus 12:49

Apparently Islamists agree with Germany, France, and Britain that multiculturalism is a weakening influence.

Therefore, for Mr. Awad's benefit, America needs to insure that there are no laws preventing him from emigrating from any one of the United States to a nation offering sharia law that could maximize his life's ambitions.

Lastly, most believe that the majority of Muslim Americans are as far removed from the worldwide Islamic agenda as the majority of Christians are from the ecumenical agenda of the World Council of Churches.

America's Vision vs. God's Standard of Justice

Power Struggles Continue

Power struggles are not new. The first such instance was between God and His created being, Lucifer, son of the morning. Notice the excessive use of the personal pronoun 'I' in Lucifer's following proclamation.

"You said in your heart, 'I will ascend to heaven; I will raise my throne above the stars of God...I will ascend above the tops of the clouds; I will make myself like the Most High.'" Isaiah 14:13-14

The Bible is very clear concerning God's reaction to Lucifer's prideful intentions and rhetoric.

"But you are brought down to the grave, to the depths of the pit." Isaiah 14:15

When the Assyrian king Sennacherib was planning to overrun Jerusalem during the reign of King Hezekiah of Judah he took full credit for his imperialistic endeavors and spoke boastfully about his powers.

"...I have ascended the heights of the mountains...I have cut down its tallest cedars...I have reached its remotest parts...I have dug wells in foreign lands...I have dried up all the streams of Egypt." 2 Kings 19:23-24

But the king of Assyria was rebuked, in fact laughed at, by Israel's God who reminded Sennacherib that He, God, was using Sennacherib to perform His plan. When world leaders attribute their successes to their own doing, they will be deposed in God's time.

"The Virgin Daughter of Zion despises you and mocks you. The Daughter of Jerusalem tosses her head as you flee. Who is it you have insulted and blasphemed? Against

whom have you raised your voice and lifted your eyes in pride? Against the Holy One of Israel! ...Because you rage against me and you insolence has reached my ears, I will put my hook in your nose and my bit in your mouth, and I will make you return by the way you came." 2 Kings 19:21-22, 28

Following the Assyrian empire appeared the Babylonian empire and king Nebuchadnezzar who made an image of gold representing his own greatness and required everyone to fall down to worship his image. Anyone who refused to do so was to be cast into the midst of a burning fiery furnace. We all know the rest of that story. Recall Nebuchadnezzar was humiliated by being consigned to eat grass like oxen until he acknowledged the sovereignty of God.

"...so that the living may know that the Most High is sovereign over the kingdoms of men and gives them to anyone he wishes and sets over them the lowest of men." Daniel 4:17b

The Roman military governor Pilate provided a vivid New Testament example of self exaltation.

"Pilate said (to Jesus). 'Don't you realize I have power either to free you or to crucify you?' Jesus answered, 'You would have no power over me if it were not given to you from above.'" John 19:10-11

Acknowledging the sovereignty of God according to the Bible has been an issue throughout the ages. There are those who put forward their own agenda without first consulting Biblical teachings.

Such occurrences are also marked by the excessive use of the personal pronoun 'I'. A profound example was seen in our president's 'new beginning' address to the Muslim world in Cairo in 2009.

- I have come here to seek a new beginning between the United States and Muslims around the world…
- I also know civilization's debt to Islam…
- I know, too, that Islam has always been a part of America's story…
- I consider it part of my responsibility…to fight against negative stereotypes of Islam wherever they appear…
- I made clear that America is not – and never will be – at war with Islam…
- I know there has been controversy about the promotion of democracy…let it be clear; no system of government can or should be imposed upon one nation by any other…
- I am committed to working with American Muslims…it is important for Western countries to avoid impeding Muslim citizens from practicing religion as they see fit…
- I saw it firsthand as a child in Indonesia, Islam has a proud tradition of tolerance…
- I am a Christian…

It is clear that President Obama believes that Christianity and Islam are not only compatible, but are in fact synergistic. We need to accept that our president means well, however, many believe that he ascribes more power and wisdom to himself than Biblically warranted. We also need to remember that God sets over kingdoms whomever He chooses to fulfill His purpose.

"...for there is no authority except that which God has established. The authorities that exist have been established by God." Romans 13:1

There is little question that President Obama is a strong willed individual. Time will tell if history will repeat itself.

VII) Specific Examples of Biblical Contradiction

The Biblical Perspective of the Pro-choice, Pro-life Debate

Perhaps the most passionate division between political ideologies is the pro-choice, pro-life debate.

The pro-choice argument advocates, favors, or supports the (legal) right of women to control their own bodies by choosing whether or not to continue a pregnancy to term.

Pro-life on the other hand advocates the (legal) protection of human fetuses…by outlawing abortion on the grounds that it is the taking of a human life.

The Bible reveals that many significant people were pre-named before their birth, or even their conception. The primary example was Jesus Himself.

"You will be with child and give birth to a son, and you are to give him the name Jesus." Luke 1:31

The conception and birth of Jesus was the culmination of an earthly genealogy first announced in Genesis.

"And I will put enmity between you and the woman, and between your offspring and hers (her seed)…" Genesis 3:15

Several examples of the family tree of Jesus are provided in the Bible.

"Isaac prayed to the LORD on behalf of his wife, because she was barren. The LORD answered his prayer, and his wife Rebekah became pregnant. The babies jostled each other within her...When the time came for her to give birth, there were twin boys in her womb." Genesis 25:21-22, 24

The Hebrew base for 'boys' in the above scripture is *Ben* defined as a son, child, or young one. And the Hebrew base for 'womb' is *Beten* meaning belly, within, or inmost part. In other words, Rebekah had two living sons within her body. One of those sons was subsequently named Jacob who was later renamed 'Israel'.

Jacob had twelve sons, one who was named Judah. The Bible presents a detailed account of Judah's offspring through his incestuous relationship with his daughter-in-law Tamar.

"When the time came for her to give birth, there were twin boys in her womb. As she was giving birth, one of them put out his hand; so the midwife took a scarlet thread and tied it on his wrist and said, 'This one came out first.' But when he drew back his hand, his brother came out, and she said, 'So this is how you have broken out!' And he was named Perez." Genesis 38:27-29

Once again, the Bible describes two brothers living together in their mother's womb.

How important was it that both Rebekah and Tamar went full term with their pregnancies and delivered the children within their wombs?

"A record of the genealogy of Jesus Christ the son of David, the son of Abraham: Abraham was the father of Isaac, Isaac the father of Jacob, Jacob the father Judah and his brothers, Judah the father of Perez...whose mother was Tamar..." Matthew 1:1-3a

The lineage of Jesus was established before the foundation of the world. What would have been the consequences if any mother in the lineage had chosen to interrupt that lineage even if her pregnancy was attributable to incest?

The Bible taught that God gave Rebekah conception. This truth was also highlighted later in the story of Ruth.

"So Boaz took Ruth and she became his wife. Then he went to her, and the LORD enabled her to conceive, and she gave birth to a son." Ruth 4:13

Her son was Obed who was the grandfather of King David. Boaz and Obed are also listed in the genealogy of Jesus.

"...Boaz the father of Obed, whose mother was Ruth, Obed the father of Jesse, and Jesse the father of King David." Matthew 1:5b-6a

Another example of one being pre-named is John the Baptist.

"But the angel said to him: 'Do not be afraid, Zechariah; your prayer has been heard. Your wife Elizabeth will bear you a son, and you are to give him the name John'...After this his wife Elizabeth became pregnant..." Luke 1:13, 24

Apparently John, while still in his mother's womb, was aware of his surroundings:

"As soon as the sound of your greeting reached my ears, the baby in my womb leaped for joy." Luke 1:44

There are others pre-named in the Bible as far as 400 years before they were born.

An interesting question arises from this discussion, i.e. why is the percent of professed Christians different than the percent of professed proponents of pro-life?

Defense of Marriage Act

Nearly two decades ago congress passed the Defense of Marriage Act by large margins in both the House of Representatives and Senate. Section 3 of this law reads in part... "The word 'marriage' means only a legal union between one man and one woman as husband and wife, and the word 'spouse' refers only to a person of the opposite sex who is a husband or a wife." This section of the law was ruled unconstitutional by a federal district court judge in July 2010.

Now during a time of extreme world unrest and unprecedented domestic fiscal upheaval, President Obama without judicial proceedings decided that section 3 of the law was indeed unconstitutional and he would not support its enforcement. His decision was announced by Attorney General Holder in that same year while the judicial ruling was still in the appeal process.

The present purpose is not to discuss the gay issue, but rather to illustrate how our leaders are handling the issue.

Marriage is clearly defined in the Bible.

"So God created man in his own image, in the image of God he created him; male and female he created them. God blessed them and said to them 'Be fruitful and increase in number; fill the earth and subdue it...' For this reason a

man will leave his father and mother and be united to his wife, and they will become one flesh." Genesis 1:27-28, 2:24

This definition of marriage was repeated by Jesus in the Gospels and reaffirmed by Paul in the Epistles.

But progressivism entered the arena and its proponents recognized the fact that the 'social landscape has changed'; subsequently President Obama urged congress to repeal 'don't ask, don't tell'. In 2009 Obama addressed the Human Rights Campaign and stated the following:

"My expectation is that when you look back on these years, you will see a time in which we put a stop to discrimination against gays and lesbians – whether in the office or on the battlefield. You will see a time in which we as a nation finally recognize relationships between two men or two women are just as real and admirable as a relationship between a man and a woman. You will see a nation that's valuing and cherishing these families as we build a more perfect union – a union in which gay Americans are an important part. I am committed to these goals. And my administration will continue fighting to achieve them."

Well he is certainly living up to his promises. Not only is his stance anti-Biblical, he is involving the federal government which means all tax paying citizens will help fund such activity.

The General Accounting Office has identified over 1,100 statuary provisions related to marital status. Such protection and rights include filing status for income tax, federal estate tax rules, Social Security survivor benefits, federal Family Medical Leave Act benefits, federal and state laws applying to pension plans, employer provided health insurance plans, etc. These items will place additional financial burdens on tax payers.

But the most significant aspect of all this is that decisions are being made by our Federal Government that protects and reward people for breaking God's laws.

"Woe to those who call evil good and good evil, who put darkness for light and light for darkness, who put bitter for sweet and sweet for bitter. Woe to those who are wise in their own eyes and clever in their own sight." Isaiah 5:20-21

Many have speculated that President Obama made this decision for political reasons, i.e. to build his base for 2012 inasmuch as his campaign rhetoric reflected his then contradictory opinion that marriage was strictly between one man and one woman. If his recent decision was in fact political another applicable verse could be added.

"Woe to those...who acquit the guilty for a bribe, but deny justice to the innocent." Isaiah 5:22a-23

Progressives may mean well, however, while manmade laws may change to keep pace with societal trends, the word of God is immutable and remains the benchmark for this nation's 'sure to come' reckoning.

It is not hard to understand why only one third of Americans believe their president is a Christian.

So while our president condemns Israelis for building housing units in their own land, he advocates the breaking of God's basic laws and protection of the offenders. Once again, what in the world are we thinking?

Best Provider – Government or God?

Many think of God as the sovereign God of the universe and the Savior of the soul, but seldom think of Him being involved in economic issues. Very little is said about God as being the answer to the economic woes presently being experienced by this great nation, and in fact around the world.

The Bible, however, isn't silent on the issue but does in fact say much about both the macro and micro economic benefits of looking to God for solutions. When God chose Israel to be the model nation for all the earth, He listed in great detail the economic benefits He would provide, but with certain stipulations.

"These are the commands, decrees and laws the LORD your God directed me to teach you to observe in the land that you are crossing the Jordan to possess, so that you, your children and their children after them may fear the LORD your God as long as you live by keeping all his decrees and commands..." Deuteronomy 6:1-2

Recall that Paul in the New Testament stated that what happened to Israel as a nation was to serve as examples for this present age.

Many do in fact compare Israel's gifted land to America breaking their ties with Britain and traveling west for a new beginning; however, America will never achieve the status of Israel. America's role is to support Israel and help her live up to and fulfill God's expectations for her.

"When the LORD your God brings you into the land he swore to your fathers, to Abraham, Isaac and Jacob,

to give you – a land with large, flourishing cities you did not build, houses filled with all kinds of good things you did not provide, wells you did not dig, and vineyards and olive groves you did not plant – then when you eat and are satisfied, be careful that you do not forget the LORD, who brought you out of Egypt, out of the land of slavery." Deuteronomy 6:10-12

The above passage contains several significant points. The immutable promise was for Abraham's offspring through Isaac and Jacob. God would give riches to Israel for which they did not labor.

Then the Bible continues to list more of what God would provide for Israel.

"For the LORD your God is bringing you into a good land – a land with streams and pools of water, with springs flowing in the valleys and hills; a land with wheat and barley, vines and fig trees, pomegranates, olive oil and honey; a land where bread will not be scarce and you will lack nothing..." Deuteronomy 8:7-9a

The land would provide food 'without scarcity' so Israel wouldn't need to depend on any other nation for its sustenance. But that's not all.

"...a land where the rocks are iron and you can dig copper out of the hills." Deuteronomy 8:9b

The land would also provide natural resources to be mined and used for other needs without, once again, depending on others.

Well, so far so good, God would provide for Israel's needs, but how about the ability to prosper over and above the necessities?

"But remember the LORD your God, for it is he who gives you the ability to produce wealth..." Deuteronomy 8:18

The Obama administration believes that everyone should share equally in a nation's wealth. However, Solomon was given extraordinary wealth by God, and on the other hand:

"The poor you will always have with you, but you will not always have me." Matthew 26:11

Thus the scriptures reveal that God deals with individuals as well as nations and is intimately involved in each individual's role in the total picture.

And lastly, what stipulations does God place on a nation in order to receive His bountiful provisions?

"Be careful that you do not forget the LORD your God, failing to observe his commands, his laws and his decrees..." Deuteronomy 8:11

If the Bible is true, and if in fact America is a Christian nation, why aren't these great truths part of the political rhetoric, especially during election seasons?

We're missing a grand opportunity.

VIII) Summary Thoughts

Who Should We Believe?

Recall from Jewish history that the Jews became disenchanted with the governance of the Judges who ruled over them and they made known to Samuel the prophet that they wanted to be just like all the other nations, i.e. they wanted to be ruled by a king. They wanted change.

Therefore, God in His sovereignty provided Israel with a king. Israel's first king was Saul who subsequently lost his kingship due to disobedience of God's instructions.

The Bible is not silent about kingdoms or nations going past the point of no return regarding pending judgment. The major cause of such judgment is abandoning God's word. The Prophet Jeremiah writes about Judah's apostasy:

"Although our sins testify against us, O LORD, do something for the sake of your name...do not forsake us! ...Then the LORD said to me (Jeremiah), 'Do not pray for the well-being of this people...Instead I will destroy them with the sword, famine and plague.'" Jeremiah 14:7, 9, 11-12

Now fast forward to the present. The United States was very dissatisfied with President George Bush and clamored for change. The majority of voters did in fact vote for change and elected Barack Obama for president.

Those ungrateful 'right wingers' now say that America, under President Obama's leadership is in a state of rapid decline and is headed for disaster. Is America heading for prosperity or disaster?

Of course it depends on who is asked. There is a book authored by Peter Diamandis entitled: 'The Future is Better than you Think'. The book is very popular.

Then there is Pat Buchanan's latest book entitled: 'The Suicide of a Superpower'. The book extends the trend lines of America's history and the current political climate and takes the reader right up to Revelation chapter 18, i.e. the fall of materialism. The book is well researched and contains over 1100 reference notes.

Buchanan's thesis on America's decline is traced to several historic changes: 'America's loss of her cradle faith, Christianity; the moral, social, and cultural collapse that have followed from that loss; and the slow death of the people who created and ruled the nation.'

The content of Buchanan's book was the reason he was fired from his association with MSNBC. In other words, he was fired for telling the truth.

Consider further that President Obama in one of his State of the Union addresses proclaimed boldly:

"America is back and anyone who says America is in decline doesn't know what they're talking about."

So once again, everyone has the freedom to choose to either place their hope in Diamandis' optimistic view of the future and the President's assessment of reality, or in Buchanan's view based on historical trends, current political priorities, and Bible prophecy.

Who Will Have the Last Laugh?

Laughter in the Bible is recorded way back in the time of Abraham. Recall when God told Abraham and Sarah that they would have a child when Sarah was well past normal child bearing years, both of them laughed at the idea. History records that God's promise was fulfilled with the birth of Isaac at the exact time foretold.

Recall also that Abraham and Sarah had intervened in an attempt to fulfill God's plan as Sarah offered her maidservant Hagar to Abraham to fulfill God's promise of a son which would be the seed of Abraham's own body.

The result was the birth of Ishmael. Subsequently there was animosity between Sarah and her maidservant Hagar from the time of Ishmael's birth. There was also animosity between their sons Ishmael and Isaac. Such animosity is very much alive today.

The Bible reveals that at Isaac's weaning celebration when Ishmael was in his early teen years he laughed at the young child Isaac.

"The child (Isaac) grew and was weaned, and on the day Isaac was weaned Abraham held a great feast. But Sarah saw that the son (Ishmael) whom Hagar the Egyptian had borne to Abraham was mocking (scoffing)..." Genesis 21:8-9

The Hebrew for 'mock' has several synonyms including laugh, scoff, scorn, deride, or make sport.

Later in the Psalms David wrote about the suffering of the future Messiah who would be of the lineage of Abraham, Isaac, Jacob...and David. While suffering on the cross David's offspring would also be mocked and scorned.

"All who see me mock me; they hurl insults, shaking their heads: 'He trusts in the LORD; let the LORD rescue him. Let him deliver him, since he delights in him.'" Psalm 22:7-8

A millennium later that prophecy was perfectly fulfilled.

"The people stood watching, and the rulers even sneered at him. They said, 'He saved others; let him save himself if he is the Christ of God, the Chosen One.' The soldiers also came up and mocked him...and said, 'If you are the king of the Jews, save yourself.'" Luke 23:35-37

Therefore, God's chosen descendant of Abraham to receive the covenant, namely Isaac, was laughed at, mocked and scorned and Jesus the Son of God through Isaac was also laughed at, mocked and scorned.

But the issue of laughter is far from over.

The Psalmist once again addresses the issue of laughter.

"The kings of the earth take their stand and the rulers gather together against the LORD and against his Anointed One. 'Let us break their chains,' they say, 'and throw off their fetters.' The One enthroned in heaven laughs; the Lord scoffs at them. Then he rebukes them in his anger..." Psalm 2:2-5a

Notice who will be doing the laughing and deriding in the future. The former object of scorn and mocking will be doing the laughing.

The Bible in fact reveals that all who reject wisdom, which is embodied in Christ and offered freely, will partake of God's derision.

"But since you rejected me when I called and no one gave heed when I stretched out my hand, since you ignored all my advice and would not accept my rebuke, I in turn will laugh at your disaster; I will mock when calamity overtakes you – when calamity overtakes you like a storm, when disaster sweeps over you like a whirlwind, when distress and trouble overwhelm you." Proverbs 1:24-27

It is so easy to focus on the love of God that many times we overlook the fact that the final book in the Bible focuses on the wrath of God that befalls on all who take lightly the promises made through Abraham, Isaac, and Jacob.

And so it is, the One who was/is laughed at, mocked and scorned will unquestionably have the last laugh.

CHAPTER 5

DEALING WITH CONTEMPORARY PHARISEES

THE JEWISH SECT called the Pharisees originated after the Jews returned to Judea upon their freedom from their Babylonian captivity. The timing would have been approximately five centuries before the birth of Christ.

Inasmuch as the doctrine of the Pharisees was so significant during the time of Christ's earthly ministry, logic suggests there would be an application for current times. And so it is, the doctrine of the Pharisees is widely present today and aptly describes those who oppose and suppress the doctrines and teachings of Christ.

Such thinking defines the major issues confronting both the church and state today.

This chapter will address pharisaic thinking that pervades contemporary culture. We'll see that such thinking is as dangerous in our present culture as it was during Jesus' original time on earth.

Doctrine of the Pharisees

The Pharisees added many 'traditions' to the Jewish law claiming such traditions were derived from the same official law delivered to Moses on Mount Sinai. Such traditions were self serving with the primary purpose to set the Pharisees apart as elitists and holier than the common Jewish person. The Pharisees taught that their 'traditions of the elders' carried the same weight as the true Mosaic Law.

Their main problem was that they could not accept the New Covenant and continued to teach adamantly that salvation was still partially based on obeying the law and their Jewish heritage. In other words they could not accept that salvation was a matter of faith alone.

During Jesus' earthly ministry the Pharisees constantly questioned and opposed His authority and His teachings.

"And the Pharisees and the scribes asked Him, 'Why do Your disciples not walk according to the tradition of the elders...' And He said to them 'Rightly did Isaiah prophesy of you hypocrites...THIS PEOPLE HONORS ME WITH THEIR LIPS, BUT THEIR HEART IS FAR AWAY FROM ME. BUT IN VAIN DO THEY WORSHIP ME, TEACHING AS DOCTRINES THE PRECEPTS OF MEN.'" Mark 7:5-7

Then Jesus summarized the discussion by revealing the unintended consequences of such thinking.

"Neglecting the commandment of God, you hold to the tradition of men...thus invalidating the word of God by your tradition which you have handed down; and you do many things such as that." Mark 7:8a, 13

The significance of this issue cannot be over emphasized. Men invented self-serving ordinances and attributed to them the same weight as God's laws. Such a practice in effect made 'the word of God of no effect' or basically nullifying God's word.

It can be compared to current policies that contradict God's precepts such as being a debtor to other nations. Pharisaic thinking is the basis of the practice of drafting and approving legislation that protects those who break God's laws.

During the early days of the church many Jews would not abandon tradition or ritualism.

"And some men came down from Judea and began teaching the brethren, 'Unless you are circumcised according to the custom of Moses, you cannot be saved.'" Acts 15:1

The issues of traditionalism and ritualism were several of Paul's major obstructions in growing the church.

"Behold I, Paul, say to you that if you receive circumcision, Christ will be of no benefit to you. And I testify again to every man who receives circumcision, that he is under obligation to keep the whole Law." Galatians 5:2-3

Paul's response was that if anyone depended on the law to save him they must obey the whole law which is, of course, impossible.

Paul taught consistently that depending on works for salvation is deception of Satan. He consistently taught that Christ alone was sufficient.

"See to it that no one takes you captive through philosophy and empty deception, according to the tradition of men, according to the elementary principles of the world, rather than according to Christ. For in Him all the fullness of Deity dwells in bodily form, and in Him you have been made complete......" Colossians 2:8-10a

Paul's argument was and is the basis of Christian doctrine.

Pharisees – Masters of Political Correctness

The Pharisees began their assault on grace during Jesus' ministry by dismissing the message of repentance by John the Baptist. They thought they were saved and sanctified due to their heritage.

"And when all the people and the tax-gatherers heard this, they acknowledged God's justice, having been baptized with the baptism of John. But the Pharisees and lawyers rejected God's purpose for themselves, not having been baptized by John." Luke 7:29-30

The Pharisees were self righteous and outwardly moral. Their appearance was deceiving. Jesus warned His disciples about them repeatedly.

"And He also told this parable to certain ones who trusted in themselves... 'Two men went up into the temple to pray, one a Pharisee, and the other a tax-gatherer. The Pharisee stood and was praying thus to himself, God, I thank Thee that I am not like other people: swindlers, unjust, adulterers, or even like this tax-gatherer.'" Luke 18:9-11

The tax collector, however, recognized his helplessness and begged for mercy.

"...God, be merciful to me the sinner!' Luke 18:13b

Jesus summarized His parable by comparing the self righteous with the one who confessed his sin.

"I tell you, this man went down to his house justified rather than the other; for everyone who exalts himself shall be humbled, but he who humbles himself shall be exalted." Luke 18:14

The Pharisees never seemed to recognize the similarities between self righteousness and depravation.

The Pharisees sought recognition and approval from other men. They were entirely politically correct in this manner.

"Then Jesus spoke to the multitudes and to His disciples, saying, 'The scribes and the Pharisees have seated themselves in the chair of Moses; therefore all that they tell you, do and observe, but do not do according to their deeds; for they say things, and do not do them. And they tie up heavy loads, and lay them on men's shoulders; but they themselves are unwilling to move them with so much as a finger. But they do all their deeds to be noticed by men...'" Matthew 24:1-5

Jesus said to the people to do as they were instructed by the scribes if it was truly in accordance with the Mosaic Law. That was the basic duty of the scribes to interpret the law to the people.

But then the Pharisees gave instructions for the people to also obey their traditions which they themselves had no intention of doing. Jesus told the people to ignore such instructions.

It reminds one of our 'regulation nation' and the Affordable Care Act in which the drafters are exempt from its requirements.

But note in particular the last part of the above scripture passage, i.e. 'all their works they do to be seen by men.'

Paul, once again, addressed that very issue.

For am I now seeking the favor of men, or of God? Or am I striving to please men? If I were still trying to please men, I would not be a bond-servant of Christ. For I would have you know, brethren, that the gospel which was preached by me is not according to man." Galatians 1:10-11

Paul taught that the choice to please men or God is mutually exclusive, i.e. one cannot have it both ways. He stated that if his teaching was for the purpose of pleasing men, he would be forfeiting his relationship to Christ.

Paul taught a similar message to the church at Thessalonica.

"...but just as we have been approved by God to be entrusted with the gospel, so we speak, not as pleasing men but God, who examines our hearts. For we never came with flattering speech, as you know, nor with a pretext for greed...nor did we seek glory from men, either from you or from others, even though as apostles of Christ we might have asserted our authority."

1 Thessalonians 2:4-6

And then it can't be overlooked that the Pharisees loved money.

"Now the Pharisees, who were lovers of money, were listening to all these things, and they were scoffing at Him. And He said to them, 'You are those who justify yourselves

in the sight of men, but God knows your hearts; for that which is highly esteemed among men is detestable in the sight of God.'" Luke 16:14-15

Thus it can be seen that the Pharisees were/are more interested in pleasing men than God.

The Pharisees' False Security

The Pharisees placed their security in their heritage and their salvation by works. As descendants of Abraham, the Pharisees felt safe and secure.

"They (Pharisees) answered Him, 'We are Abraham's offspring, and have never yet been enslaved to anyone;' how is it that You say, 'You shall become free?'" John 8:33

Jesus acknowledged their claim, but set them straight in their thinking.

"I know that you are Abraham's offspring; yet you seek to kill Me, because My word has no place in you. I speak the things which I have seen with My Father; therefore you also do the things which you heard from your father." John 8:37-38

The Pharisees persisted in the argument that Abraham was their father and therefore they were safe and beyond reproach. They advanced the argument by claiming that God Himself was their Father.

"Jesus said to them, 'If God were your Father, you would love Me; for I proceeded forth and have come from God...Why do you not understand what I am saying? ...You are of your father the devil, and you want to do the desires of your father...'" John 8:42-44

There are yet today many modern day Pharisees who still believe that being the physical descendants of Abraham is sufficient for salvation. Paul confronted that same argument as he wrote to the Christians in Rome.

"What then shall we say that Abraham, our forefather according to the flesh, has found? For if Abraham was justified by works, he has something to boast about... For what does the Scriptures say? 'AND ABRAHAM BELIEVED GOD, AND IT WAS RECKONED TO HIM AS RIGHTEOUSNESS.'" Romans 4:1-3

Abraham was indeed justified, or deemed righteous before God, but not by obeying the law (which no man could do) but rather by taking God at His word. He believed in that which God had promised even though he hadn't seen the proof of the promise.

If he had indeed fulfilled the law then he really would have had something to boast about!

The sum of the matter is that one is saved by believing the latest and final revelation of God which in this generation is Christ, the only one capable of fulfilling the complete law.

Paul then makes the issue more clearly by specifying which of Abraham's lineage will inherit the promise of salvation. In other words, not all of Abraham's descendants will receive the ultimate promise.

"...For they are not all Israel who are descended from Israel; neither are they all children because they are Abraham's descendants, but: 'THROUGH ISAAC YOUR DESCENDANTS WILL BE NAMED.' That is, it is not the children of the flesh who are children of God, but the

children of the promise are regarded as descendants." Romans 9:6b-8

Subsequently Paul explained in more detail the difference between those born under the promise and those born under the law, or works.

"Tell me, you who want to be under law, do you not listen to the law? For it is written that Abraham had two sons, one by the bondwoman and one by the free woman. But the son by the bondwoman was born according to the flesh (law), and the son by the free woman through the promise."
Galatians 4:21-23

Paul goes on to describe the two sons.

"And you brethren, like Isaac, are children of promise. But as at that time he who was born according to the flesh persecuted him who was born according to the Spirit, so it is now also. But what does the Scripture say? 'CAST OUT THE BONDWOMAN AND HER SON, FOR THE SON OF THE BONDWOMAN SHALL NOT BE AN HEIR WITH THE SON OF THE FREE WOMAN.' So then, brethren, we are not children of a bondwoman, but of the free woman."
Galatians 4:28-31

This extremely profound passage clarifies the teaching of the two original sons of Abraham.

"But God said, 'No, but Sarah your wife shall bear you a son, and you shall call his name Isaac; and I will establish My covenant with him for an everlasting covenant for his descendants after him." Genesis 17:19

The Pharisees of Jesus' time apparently did not understand the Genesis account or the significance of the two brothers. Modern day Pharisees are basically the same as their first century counterparts, i.e. confidence in salvation by works.

The Pharisees' Ultimate Sin

The Pharisees were the epitome of pride and self righteousness; however, their ultimate sin was willfully rejecting the deity of Jesus and attributing to Satan His power to perform miracles.

After Jesus explained His deity to the Pharisees, they attempted to stone Him for blasphemy.

"Jesus said to them, 'Truly, truly, I say to you, before Abraham was born, I AM.' Therefore they picked up stones to throw at Him..." John 8:58-59a

The Pharisees' rejection of Jesus' claim to deity was shared by other members of the Sanhedrin including the high priest.

Other incidents of rejection of Jesus' claim to deity include:

"For this cause therefore the Jews were seeking all the more to kill Him, because He...was calling God His own Father, making Himself equal with God." John 5:18

The more miracles that Jesus performed, the more the Pharisees hated Him and were afraid for their own standing among the people.

"Then there was brought to Him a demon-possessed man who was blind and dumb, and He healed him, so that the dumb man spoke and saw. And all the multitudes were amazed..." Matthew 12:22-23a

America's Vision vs. God's Standard of Justice

The Pharisees were running out of contrived reasons for Jesus' miracles and hit rock bottom.

"But when the Pharisees heard it, they said, 'This man casts out demons only by Beelzebub the ruler of the demons.'" Matthew 12:24

Jesus calmly and quickly placed the argument squarely on the Pharisees' shoulders.

"And knowing their thoughts He said to them, 'Any kingdom divided against itself is laid waste; and any city or house divided against itself shall not stand. And if Satan casts out Satan, he is divided against himself; how then shall his kingdom stand?'" Matthew 12:25-26

The Pharisees could not respond to the truth of Jesus' reasoning. Then Jesus confronted the Pharisees with the sin of sins.

"Therefore I say to you, any sin and blasphemy shall be forgiven men, but blasphemy against the Spirit shall not be forgiven. And whoever shall speak a word against the Son of Man, it shall be forgiven him; but whoever shall speak against the Holy Spirit, it shall not be forgiven him, either in this age, or in the age to come." Matthew 12:31-32

The sin of the Pharisees was that they had witnessed first hand the power of the Holy Spirit manifested in Christ and demonstrated by His miracles, but they rejected the truth. They didn't reject the truth in ignorance, but rather with conscious choice, thereby committing the ultimate sin.

The major goal of the Pharisees was to get rid of Jesus. It appeared that after every miracle the Pharisees were of one mind.

"But the Pharisees went out, and counseled together against Him, as to how they might destroy Him." Matthew 12:14

Just prior to Jesus being sent to Pilate for interrogation, Jesus was interrogated by the high priest.

"...Again the high priest was questioning Him, and saying to Him, 'Are You the Christ, the Son of the Blessed One?' And Jesus said, 'I am...' And tearing his clothes, the high priest said, 'What further need do we have of witnesses? You have heard the blasphemy...' And they all condemned Him to be deserving of death." Mark 14:61-64

The irony, of course, was that the Pharisees and high priest were committing the same sin that they were accusing Jesus of committing.

The reason that the Pharisees wanted to kill Jesus was not only because of alleged blasphemy, but rather for their own self preservation. They could see their power base falter.

"And when the chief priests and the Pharisees heard His parables, they understood that He was speaking about them. And when they sought to seize Him, they became afraid of the multitudes, because they held Him to be a prophet." Matthew 21:45-46

Jesus' Denunciation of the Pharisees

Prior to Jesus denouncing the Pharisees for their misguided ideology and theology, He clearly declared to the multitude that the Pharisees had totally missed the mark relative to the meaning of righteousness.

"For I say to you, that unless your righteousness surpasses that of the scribes and Pharisees, you shall not enter the kingdom of heaven." Matthew 5:20

Jesus later admonished His disciples to beware of the doctrine of the Pharisees.

"He began saying to His disciples first of all, 'Beware of the leaven of the Pharisees, which is hypocrisy.'" Luke 12:1b

Then Jesus gave very specific examples of the hypocrisy of the Pharisees and summarily denounced them.

"Woe to you, scribes and Pharisees, hypocrites, because you devour widows' houses, even while for a pretense you make long prayers..." Matthew 23:14

The Pharisees took advantage of widows by telling them they would serve God better by giving their inheritance from their husbands to the temple service.

"Woe to you, blind guides, who say, 'Whoever swears by the temple, that is nothing; but whoever swears by the gold in the temple, he is obligated.' You fools and blind men; which is more important, the gold, or the temple that sanctifies the gold?" Matthew 23:16-17

The gold was tangible and measurable while no man could be held accountable for the temple and therefore the oath was not binding. This tactic of the Pharisees provided the opportunity to make oaths or promises that they had no intention of honoring.

Jesus then denounced the Pharisees for misguided priorities.

"Woe to you, scribes and Pharisees, hypocrites! For you tithe mint and dill and cumin, and have neglected the

weightier provisions of the law: justice and mercy and faithfulness; but these are the things you should have done without neglecting the others. You blind guides, who strain out a gnat and swallow a camel!" Matthew 23:23-24

The Pharisees focused on the visible and minor aspects of the law. They did well to do those things, but they should not have avoided the major less visible spirit of the law.

"Woe to you, scribes and Pharisees, hypocrites! For you clean the outside of the cup and of the dish, but inside they are full of robbery and self-indulgence. You blind Pharisee, first clean the inside of the cup and of the dish, so that the outside of it may become clean also." Matthew 23:25-26

The Pharisees were again concerned with what was visible so as to be considered religious. Their real motives and thoughts were hidden. They were pretentious.

"Woe to you, scribes and Pharisees, hypocrites! For you are like whitewashed tombs which on the outside appear beautiful, but inside they are full of dead men's bones and all uncleanness. Even so you too outwardly appear righteous to men, but inwardly you are full of hypocrisy and lawlessness." Matthew 23:27-28

Then Jesus really condemned the Pharisees for being as lawless as those who killed the prophets sent to Israel before them.

"Woe to you, scribes and Pharisees, hypocrites! For you build the tombs of the prophets and adorn the monuments of the righteous, and say, 'If we had been living in the days of our fathers, we would not have been partners with them in shedding the blood of the prophets.'" Matthew 23:29-30

"Consequently you bear witness against yourselves, that you are sons of those who murdered the prophets." Matthew 23:31

But one of the greatest condemnations of the Pharisees was that their message prevented others from learning the truth.

"But woe to you, scribes and Pharisees, hypocrites, because you shut off the kingdom of heaven from men; for you do not enter in yourselves, nor do you allow those who are entering to go in." Matthew 23:13

Contemporary Pharisees

Modern day Pharisees are alive and active around the globe and still do the same things that Jesus denounced in His day. Recall that Jesus warned His disciples of the Pharisees and told them to beware of their doctrines and teachings. The Greek base for 'beware' means more than just to take heed or be on guard, but it also means 'not to do' as they do.

The same warning is in effect today. No nation is presently exempt from the doctrine of the Pharisees.

The Pharisees of today are also self-righteous and still believe that salvation is based on personal effort and heritage. As such they reject grace based on the vicarious death of Jesus on the cross. Pharisees have never realized that the law, which no man could obey, was fulfilled by Christ.

The Pharisees added countless rules to the law of God which they claimed carried the same weight as the Law of Moses. Such additional rules were labeled 'traditions of the elders'. The Pharisees insisted that others follow such traditions while they exempted themselves from doing so.

Because such rules often superseded the God-given law, Jesus said that such laws 'made the Law of God of no effect'.

Such contemporary 'laws' often protect the 'rights' of those who reject Christ and all He represents. A common example would be the legal right to kill children while they are being protected and perfected in their mother's womb.

Pharisees of today are hypocritical, proud, and pretentious and are more interested in outward appearances than inward humility. Efforts to please men are more important to them than pleasing God. Current day Pharisees make decisions and draft legislation based on polls. They are the epitome of political correctness.

They will often publicly voice their change of positions of significant issues based solely on appeasing the electorate.

They will take credit for acts over which they have little or no control. Their speech is recognized by the excessive use of the personal pronoun 'I'.

Pharisees did and do make phony oaths to impress others but which they often have no intention or power of keeping. Such oaths provide the opportunity to avoid telling the truth.

Pharisees did and do base their security on their ancestry claiming that being the offspring of Abraham is sufficient to find favor with God. The Bible, however, refutes such claim numerous times.

"...neither are they all children because they are Abraham's descendants, but: 'THROUGH ISAAC YOUR DESCENDANTS WILL BE NAMED.'" Romans 9:7

Pharisees did and do deny the deity of Christ and the power of the Holy Spirit. The Bible is very clear on this issue. Such deniers are consigned to everlasting destruction.

Historical Pharisees were engaged in the redistribution of wealth for their own selfish purposes as evidenced by their 'devouring widow's houses'. Similarly redistribution is one of the keystone fiscal policies of this administration's current progressive agenda.

Contemporary Pharisees continue to promote unbiblical doctrines. The consequence of such practice is their denial into the kingdom of heaven. But even more serious is that their deceiving doctrines prevent others from entering.

Jesus did not mince words on this matter.

"Woe to you, scribes and Pharisees, hypocrites, because you travel about on sea and land to make one proselyte; and when he becomes one, you make him twice as much a son of hell as yourselves." Matthew 23:15

Therefore, one need only to look around and examine what is happening in this nation and the world today and compare to the immutable Biblical teachings to see how close or distant we are to God's standard of righteousness and justice. The presence of pharisaic doctrines is irrefutable.

And recall the goal of the zealous Pharisee Saul and many around the world of like mind.

"But Saul began ravaging the church..." Acts 8:3a

To accept any of the doctrines of modern day Pharisees is to reject Biblical teachings.

Modern Day Sadducees

The other major Jewish sect which was active during the first century was the Sadducees. They were very active in both religious and political issues. They were typically wealthy, aristocratic, members of the priestly tribe and generally maintained the temple during the time of Jesus' earthly ministry. High priests Annas and Caiaphas were Sadducees.

Sadducees as well as Pharisees could be part of the 71 member Sanhedrin which was in fact headed by the prevailing high priest.

Sadducees were in nearly direct opposition to the theology of the Pharisees. They were firm adherents to the Mosaic Law and the Pentateuch, but rejected the traditions of the Pharisees. The Sadducees were worldly minded and believed in complete moral freedom during one's life and rejected the doctrine of afterlife.

Jesus warned his followers to beware of the doctrine of both Pharisees and Sadducees.

"And Jesus said to them, 'Watch out and beware of the leaven of the Pharisees and Sadducees.'...Then they understood that He did not say to beware of the leaven of bread, but of the teaching of the Pharisees and Sadducees." Matthew 16:6, 12

The Sadducees and Pharisees did however, have several things in common. When John the Baptist initially confronted the Sadducees he classified them together with the Pharisees.

"But when he (John the Baptist) saw many of the Pharisees and Sadducees coming for baptism, he said to them, 'You brood of vipers, who warned you to flee from the wrath to come?'" Matthew 3:7

The term 'brood' is synonymous with offspring and the term 'viper' is synonymous with snake and serpent which means that John called them sons of the devil.

The major common issue that the Sadducees shared with the Pharisees was their hatred for Jesus. That can be easily understood seeing they were as John, and later Jesus noted, both sects of the devil.

When Jesus was taken in the Garden of Gethsemane He was brought initially before Annas and then to Caiaphas and the Sanhedrin.

"Now the chief priests and the whole Council kept trying to obtain false testimony against Jesus, in order that they might put Him to death; and they did not find it, even though many false witnesses came forward..." Matthew 26:59-60

Subsequently two false witnesses did come forward and quoted Jesus as previously saying that if the temple was destroyed He would build it up again in three days. Such testimony was just the opening that Caiaphas was looking for.

"...And the high priest said to Him, 'I adjure You by the living God, that You tell us whether You are the Christ, the Son of God.'" Matthew 26:63

"Jesus said to him, 'You have said it yourself...'" Matthew 26:64a

Caiaphas immediately responded, saying:

"...He has blasphemed! What further need do we have of witnesses? Behold, you have now heard the blasphemy; what do you think?" Matthew 26:65-66

"...They answered and said, 'He is deserving of death!' Then they spat in His face and beat Him with their fists; and others slapped Him..." Matthew 26:66b-67

The Sanhedrin had done what they set out to do. The next step was to convince the Roman government that Jesus should be put death.

"Now when morning had come, all the chief priests and the elders of the people took counsel against Jesus to put Him to death; and they bound Him, and led Him away, and delivered Him up to Pilate the governor." Matthew 27:1-2

On the day when the Passover Lamb was killed, the conversation between the Jewish leaders and Pilate came to conclusion.

"Now it was the day of preparation for the Passover; it was about the sixth hour. And he (Pilate) said to the Jews, 'Behold, your King!' They therefore cried out, 'Away with Him, away with Him, crucify Him!' Pilate said to them, 'Shall I crucify your King?' The chief priests answered, 'We have no king but Caesar.' And so he then delivered Him up to them to be crucified." John 19:14-16

Therefore, the Sadducees, as hypocritical as the Pharisees, through deceit and blasphemy, unaware they were little more than puppets, implemented that part of the master plan for Jesus established from the foundation of the world.

Suppression of Free Speech

Shortly after the beginning of the church, Peter healed a certain lame man. The healing was witnessed by many.

"And all the people saw him walking and praising God; and they were taking note of him as being the one who used to sit at the Beautiful Gate of the temple to beg alms...and they were filled with wonder and amazement at what had happened to him." Acts 3:9-10

Then Peter went on to preach to the people that the lame man was healed by faith in Jesus who had been crucified, buried, and then resurrected. He continued by stating that Jesus' suffering and death had been foretold by the prophets.

Such preaching and teaching did not set well with the Sadducees.

"And as they were speaking to the people, the priests and the captain of the temple guard, and the Sadducees, came upon them, being greatly disturbed because they were teaching the people and proclaiming in Jesus the resurrection from the dead. And they laid hands on them, and put them in jail..." Acts 4:1-3

The same ones who condemned Jesus to death demanded that Peter and John justify their authority.

"And it came about on the next day, that their rulers and elders and scribes were gathered together in Jerusalem; and Annas the high priest was there, and Caiaphas...and when they had placed them in the center, they began to inquire, 'By what power, or in what name, have you done this?'" Acts 4:5-7

Peter boldly proclaimed that their power came from the resurrected Christ.

Now when the Sadducees saw the boldness of Peter and John...they realized that they had been with Jesus. In addition they themselves had witnessed the healing of the lame man. They then sent Peter and John outside the council meeting so they could discuss the matter privately between themselves, saying:

"...What shall we do with these men? For the fact that a noteworthy miracle has taken place through them is apparent to all who live in Jerusalem and we cannot deny it. But in order that it may not spread any further among the people, let us warn them to speak no more to any man in this name." Acts 4:16-17

"And when they had summoned them, they commanded them not to speak or teach at all in the name of Jesus." Acts 4:18

However, Peter and John were not to be silenced. Being filled with the Holy Spirit they performed many miracles and drew great numbers of followers to the dismay of the Sadducees.

"But the high priest rose up, along with all his associates (that is the sect of the Sadducees), and they were filled with jealousy; and they laid hands on the apostles, and put them in a public jail." Acts 5:17-18

But an angel opened the prison doors and brought them out and instructed them to continue with their teaching and preaching. Subsequently they were recaptured and set before the Sanhedrin again.

"And when they had brought them, they stood them before the Council. And the high priest questioned them,

America's Vision vs. God's Standard of Justice

saying, 'We gave you strict orders not to continue teaching in this name, and behold, you have filled Jerusalem with your teaching, and intend to bring this man's blood upon us.'" Acts 5:27-28

But Peter and the apostles responded by saying that they ought to obey God rather than men. They had no intention of easing up on proclaiming what they had personally witnessed relative to Christ. Then they really stunned the Sanhedrin with their boldness.

"The God of our fathers raised up Jesus, whom you had put to death by hanging Him on a cross. He is the one whom God exalted to His right hand as a Prince and a Savior, to grant repentance to Israel, and forgiveness of sins. And we are witnesses of these things..." Acts 5:30-32a

Upon hearing Peter's response the council (Sanhedrin) was not only frustrated but furious. They convened again to decide how to silence Peter and the Apostles. And once again they met behind closed doors to decide on a strategy to suppress the truth.

They decided to let the new movement run its course hoping it would self-destruct as other previous insurrections.

History revealed, confirmed, and recorded the growth and permanence of the church.

So even though the formal sect of the Sadducees may have disappeared, their doctrine lives on. Many remember them for their lying, hypocrisy, and blasphemy.

The primary problem, however, with the Sadducees both then and now was/is their zealous attempts to restrict freedom of speech, especially relative to the truth of Christ and in fact all Christian doctrine.

CHAPTER SIX

THE FERTILE CRESCENT: GEOGRAPHIC CENTER OF PROPHECY

SEVERAL MILLENNIA AGO nestled in the rich Euphrates and Tigris River valley was an area called the land of Shinar. Much of that land is now known as Iraq. The land of Shinar was part of the 'Fertile Crescent' or 'Cradle of Civilization'. Present countries which are part of the Fertile Crescent include Iraq, Syria, Lebanon, Jordan, Kuwait, portions of Northern Africa (such as Egypt, Libya, and Ethiopia), portions of Southeast Turkey, portions of Western Iran, the Sinai Peninsula, and of course Israel is at the center. Located in the Eastern section of the Fertile Crescent was Mesopotamia and in Southern Mesopotamia was the land of the Chaldeans and within Chaldea was a city named Ur.

Recall that the Garden of Eden was watered by four rivers, two of which were the Euphrates and Tigris. The Euphrates River will play a major role near the end of the great tribulation period.

This area was where man's journey began and according to the Bible this is the same geographic area of focus for the return of Christ.

Also located in Mesopotamia were the city of Babylon and the Tower of Babel.

Babylon: Yesterday, Today, and Tomorrow

The name 'Babylon' in the Bible became synonymous with a place or system that was and still is void of God's word or will. It represents man's best attempts to make it on his own. Numerous times in the Bible God warns His people to flee from Babylon.

Many descendents of Noah settled in areas of the Fertile Crescent and surrounding areas. For example, sons of Japheth included Gomer, Tubal and Meshech who migrated northward into what is presently Turkey. One of Gomer's sons named Togarmah also settled in present day Turkey.

Another of Japheth's sons named Madai settled in ancient Persia, or present day Iran. Japheth's son Magog settled in an area east of present day Turkey and northwest Iran.

Noah's son Ham also had offspring including Put, Cush, Mizraim and Cannan. Put is the present day Libya, Cush is the present day Ethiopia, Mizraim is the present day Egypt, and Canaan is present day Israel.

Now Cush also had sons, one of which was named Nimrod. The Bible reveals that Nimrod's kingdom included Babel…in the land of Shinar. Nimrod and other of Noah's descendants planned to use their combined knowledge and technology to make a name for themselves without God.

"And it came about as they journeyed east, that they found a plain in the land of Shinar and settled there...And they used brick for stone, and they used tar for mortar. And they said, 'Come, let us build for ourselves a city, and a tower whose top will reach into heaven, and let us make for ourselves a name...'" Genesis 11:2-4

Such was not the will of God and He did in fact scatter the people over the face of the whole earth.

Near the end of the future tribulation period God will gather Israel's enemies together and bring them to Jerusalem, the heart of the Fertile Crescent, for a great battle.

"Behold, a day is coming for the LORD when the spoil taken from you will be divided among you, for I will gather all the nations against Jerusalem..." Zechariah 14:1-2a

Israel's enemies will be the ten horns of the kingdom prevailing at the time of Christ's return which are also the ten toes of Nebuchadnezzar's beast.

"...And I saw a beast coming up out of the sea, having ten horns and seven heads, and on his horns were ten diadems, and on his heads were blasphemous names..." Revelation 13:1

"And as the toes of the feet were partly of iron and partly of pottery, so some of the kingdom will be strong and part will be brittle." Daniel 2:42

The prophet Ezekiel identifies Israel's enemies who will participate in the great future battle.

"...set your face toward...the land of Magog...Meshech, and Tubal (all areas of Turkey)...Persia (Iran), Ethiopia, and Put (Libya) are with them...Gomer with...Beth-togarmah

(areas of Turkey) from the remote parts of the north..." Ezekiel 38:2, 5-6

Thus the land of Shinar within the Fertile Crescent is where history began for man, and it will be in the same area where God's chosen people will be restored and their adversaries destroyed.

Euphrates River: Past, Present, and Future

There are few geographical sites in the Bible more prominent than the Euphrates River. The Euphrates River is first mentioned in the second chapter of Genesis and played a significant role in world history and will figure prominently in the future.

The Euphrates River extends over 1,700 miles from the headwaters in the mountains of present day Turkey and flows south and east through Syria, Iraq, and empties into the Persian Gulf.

The Euphrates River marks the eastern boundary of Israel's Promised Land.

It is unclear just where Israel's eastern boundary will intersect the river; however, that intersection point will determine how much of present day Jordan, Syria, and Iraq will become Israel's possession.

Located just east of the River was the ancient and infamous city of Babylon. It is difficult to separate ancient Babylon from the Euphrates River. Recall the name Babylon was synonymous with evil.

It began when Abraham was told to leave his native home near the Euphrates River, travel westward, and settle in Canaan bordering the Mediterranean Sea.

The Euphrates River became a dividing line separating the 'gods' in the Fertile Crescent and the God of Abraham.

"And Joshua said to all the people, Thus says the LORD, the God of Israel, 'From ancient times your fathers lived beyond the River, namely, Terah, the father of Abraham, and they served other gods.'" Joshua 24:2

Biblical history tells of a time when Israel's King Solomon reigned over all nations from Egypt to the River Euphrates with great wisdom.

But Solomon compromised God's word and subsequently Israel was divided into north and south in 931 BC. Israel's northern tribes were overtaken by Assyria in 722 BC and southern Judah fell to Babylon in 586 BC.

The Bible reveals, however, that Israel's tribes will be reunited and her capital Jerusalem will be restored permanently in the future.

Those nations surrounding present Israel, primarily the Arab nations, and those nations east of the Euphrates River will begrudge Israel because of her favor with God. That animosity is very evident today and such animosity will increase as the time approaches for Israel to take possession of all the land promised her. Those nations east of the River will march on the Promised Land.

"And the sixth angel poured out his bowl upon the great river, the Euphrates; and its water was dried up, that the way might be prepared for the kings from the east...to gather them together for the war of the great day of God, the Almighty...to the place which in Hebrew is called Har-Magedon (Armageddon)." Revelation 16:12, 14, 16

The 'kings from the East' can be likened to the 'wise men from the East' that came to worship the Child Jesus.

"Now after Jesus was born in Bethlehem of Judea in the days of Herod the king, behold, magi from the east arrived in Jerusalem..." Matthew 2:1

The Greek meaning for *'magi'* is priests and wise men among the Medes, Persians, and Babylonians.

The Bottomless Pit: What and Where?

The bottomless pit is another name for the abyss. It is the current prison for demonic spirits and fallen angels. It is temporary in the sense that the day will come when the abyss will no longer be needed or occupied.

The same is true with hell, the temporary prison for the souls of non-repentant mankind. At the end of the millennium both the occupants of the bottomless pit and hell will be cast into the everlasting lake of fire.

It is a hard Biblical fact that occupants of both the abyss and hell have no recourse; their eternal fate is already sealed. It is interesting to note that the eternal lake of fire was prepared for the devil and his angels.

"Then He will also say to those of His left, 'Depart from Me, accursed ones, into the eternal fire which has been prepared for the devil and his angels...'" Matthew 25:41

Non-repentant mankind chooses that destiny by rejecting the provided remedy by which to avoid it.

The occupants of the abyss will be very active during the future seven year tribulation period.

The fifth and sixth trumpet judgments during the tribulation period describe some of the occupants of the abyss and their permitted activities. The ruler over those in the bottomless pit is Satan himself.

"And the fifth angel sounded, and I saw a star from heaven which had fallen to the earth; and the key of the bottomless pit was given to him." Revelation 9:1

Continuing in the same chapter of Revelation the location of the bottomless pit is revealed.

"...and I heard...one saying to the sixth angel... 'Release the four angels who are bound at the great river Euphrates.' And the four angels, who had been prepared for the hour and day and month and year, were released, so that they might kill a third of mankind." Revelation 9:13-15

So here it is seen that the River Euphrates is the location of the bottomless pit.

The Revelation further reveals that the satanically empowered anti-Christ will arise out of the bottomless pit and kill the two witnesses announced by a mighty angel.

"And when they (the two witnesses) have finished their testimony, the beast that comes up out of the Abyss will make war with them, and overcome them and kill them." Revelation 11:7

The anti-Christ is subsequently said to ascend again from the bottomless pit as he heads the ten nation federation which will make war with God's people.

"The beast that you saw was and is not, and is about to come up out of the abyss and to go to destruction." Revelation 17:8a

Subsequently the devil himself will be locked up in his own earthly prison for a thousand years.

The Bible then reveals that after the 1000 years are completed, Satan is released for a short time and given power to attempt to deceive those left on earth that had entered the millennium in natural bodies. He is swiftly destroyed.

"And the devil that deceived them was thrown into the lake of fire and brimstone, where the beast (antichrist) and the false prophet are also; and they will be tormented day and night forever and ever." Revelation 20:10

There lies ahead tremendous battles, and the area of these final battles will occur in the area where it all began, near the great river Euphrates.

Iran: Past, Present, and Future

Until about 75 years ago, Iran was known as Persia. The land was originally occupied by Madai and Elam, sons of Japheth and Shem respectively. A significant fact about Iran is that it is located east of the Euphrates River.

Iran (Persia) has a rich Biblical history as well as a profound Biblical future. The area also has a significant future according to Islamic teachings. Using both sources of information will help paint a broader picture of that geographic area and its future.

When one thinks about Iran today, their previous president Mahmoud Ahmadinejad comes to mind. He is a Shia Muslim and believes in the twelfth Imam, or the coming Islamic Mahdi. In fact he has stated publicly that he believes he has been called to usher in the Islamic savior by initiating a period of great unrest and conflict in the Middle East.

Perhaps Ahmadinejad is better known for his hatred of Israel and the great Satan, i.e. the United States of America. His agenda coincides with the Hamas charter in that it centers on the total destruction of Israel. He has no reservations about sharing his intentions.

Iran is presently developing nuclear technology and missile delivery systems. Many believe their goal is to use such technology to develop weapons to use on Israel as a means to usher in their Mahdi. The Bible also confirms Iran (Persia) will be involved in an attack on Jerusalem in the latter days. This situation is perhaps the greatest challenge facing America's foreign policy makers today.

God, however, even uses those who don't know Him to perform His will. Recall that God called the Persian King Cyrus by name 140 years before he was born to free the Jews from Babylonian captivity in 539 BC. Likewise, Ahmadinejad is in the palm of God's hand.

There is a very prolific writer and speaker on Islamic affairs named Sheikh Imran Hosein. He specializes in world economic/political issues. He recently paraphrased a profound Islamic prophecy.

"According to the prophecies of Prophet Muhammad…a non-stop army will rise from the land of Khorasan holding black flags of Islam in the end times. This army will conquer several occupied lands of Muslims till it reaches to Jerusalem. Then it will pledge its allegiance to Imam al Mahdi."

The black flags carried by Muslim armies are called 'flags of Jihad'.

Sheikh Imran Hosein went on to define the geographic area known as Khorasan. He said it included the northeast area of Iran, the northwest area of Pakistan, and all of Afghanistan. He went on to say that the British had failed in Afghanistan three times, Russia failed after a twelve year attempt, and he predicted that the United States will also fail in their attempt to change, tame, and democratize Afghanistan.

Therefore, both the Bible and Islamic teachings tell of the upcoming confrontation between the kings of the East and the future King of Jerusalem. A major difference, however, is the prophesied outcome of the conflict. Both Islam and the Bible agree there can only be one victor.

Americans have both the opportunity and responsibility to discuss such significant issues. Recall the previous Secretary of State and the head of the OIC have publicly stated that such open dialogue is healthy and will promote democracy.

Owing to the significance of Iran's present actions and the heightened violence in Afghanistan, it is believed that the current administration will 'double down' on their Middle East policy as soon as the polls indicate it would be politically expedient to do so.

Arabs and Jews will reconcile…Someday

There is perhaps no other place on earth that has such a rich history and profound future as the Middle East which includes the Garden of Eden and Babylon. That area marked the beginning of the nations and will be the area where the present age will culminate.

Israel presently occupies just a small portion of that rich land, however, the Bible reveals numerous times that Israel's borders will be expanded in the future.

"On that day the LORD made a covenant with Abram, saying 'To your descendants I have given this land, from the river of Egypt as far as the great river, the river Euphrates...'" Genesis 15:18

The area south and east of Canaan (Israel) was/is occupied by sons of Abraham including Ishmael through Hagar, sons by his subsequent wife Keturah, or other sons through concubines. The Bible reveals that Ishmael dwelt in Paran, i.e., the Sinai Peninsula, while Abraham's sons by Keturah and concubines settled east of Canaan.

"...but to the sons of his concubines, Abraham gave gifts while he was still living, and sent them away from his son Isaac eastward, to the land of the east." Genesis 25:6

There was, is, and will be conflict between the descendants of Isaac and the sons of Abraham through Hagar, Keturah, and concubines, however, the Bible tells of a future time when there will be peace between them. God described that future time to the prophet Isaiah by speaking as if addressing Zion.

"And nations will come to your light, and kings to the brightness of your rising...The wealth of the nations will come to you. A multitude of camels will cover you, the young camels of Midian and Ephah; All those from Sheba will come; They will bring gold and frankincense, and will bear good news of the praises of the LORD. All the flocks of Kedar will be gathered together to you, the rams of Nebaioth will minister to you..." Isaiah 60:3, 5-7

Isaiah mentions Midian, Ephah, and Sheba in the above passage.

"Now Abraham took another wife, whose name was Keturah. And she bore to him...Jokshan...Midian...Jokshan became the father of Sheba...and the sons of Midian were Ephah...All these were the sons of Keturah." Genesis 25:1-4

Midian, Ephah, and Sheba are located in the Arab peninsula. Sheba is presently known as Yemen. Recall the words of the Queen of Sheba to King Solomon over 3,000 years ago.

"Blessed be the LORD your God who delighted in you to set you on the throne of Israel; because the LORD loved Israel forever, therefore He made you king, to do justice and righteousness." 1 Kings 10:9

Isaiah also mentions Kedar and Nebaioth (Nebajoth).

"Now these are the records of the generations of Ishmael, Abraham's son, whom Hagar...bore to Abraham; and these are the names of the sons of Ishmael, by their names, in the order of their birth: Nebaioth...and Kedar..." Genesis 25:12-13

The Isaiah passage describes a time of peace which will follow the great tribulation. The great tribulation, also known as 'the time of Jacob's trouble' is described by Jesus:

"...for then there will be a great tribulation, such as has not occurred since the beginning of the world until now, nor ever shall be. And unless those days had been cut short, no life would have been saved; but for the sake of the elect those days shall be cut short." Matthew 24:21-22

After that time, the sons of Abraham will enjoy peace.

The Bible is not only a wonderful source of historical facts, but also the leading source of future history. It has proven to be eerily accurate; therefore, it is surprising that it is not the handbook for current foreign policy.

Time will tell whether wisdom or political correctness will prevail. Those who choose political correctness will envision Israel's land area to decrease and applaud a two state solution to resolve the Palestinian challenge prior to the tribulation.

On the other hand those who choose wisdom will see Israel's land area greatly increase and enjoy peace after the tribulation.

Legs, Feet, and Toes of Iron

There are several eschatological issues that have challenged Bible students for generations. One such challenge is the identification of the ten nation gentile federation that will exist at the return of Christ after the great tribulation.

Shortly after Judah was deported to Babylon beginning in 605 BC, the King of Babylon, Nebuchadnezzar, had a dream which he did not understand. No one could interpret the dream except the Hebrew lad Daniel. The dream was that of a large metal image of a man consisting of four metals from head to toes.

"The head of that statue was made of fine gold, its breast and its arms of silver, its belly and its thighs of bronze, its legs of iron, its feet partly of iron and partly of clay." Daniel 2:32-33

As Daniel interpreted the dream, he provided more details of the feet and toes.

"And in that you saw the feet and toes, partly of potter's clay and partly of iron, it will be a divided kingdom...and as the toes of the feet were partly of iron and partly of pottery, so some of the kingdom will be strong and part of it will be brittle." Daniel 2:41-42

Daniel revealed to Nebuchadnezzar that the gentile kingdoms of the earth would deteriorate in purity as they increased in the ability to crush opposition, i.e. the specific gravity of the metals decreased from head to toes as they increased in brittleness. Another way to view it is to consider that the autocracies became diluted with each succeeding empire.

History revealed the identity of the four world powers of Nebuchadnezzar's dream. Babylon was the head of gold, Media-Persia was the chest and arms of silver, the Greek empire was the belly and thighs of bronze, and Rome was the legs, feet, and toes of iron. These four empires ruled over Israel during their reigns.

The dream, then, reveals that at the time of the great tribulation a ten nation federation, under the rule of a future leader, will bear part of the characteristics of the original Roman Empire's strength but will be diluted by some other influence depicted by the inclusion of clay.

Part of the challenge in understanding this dream is that it depicts the Roman Empire as never being totally dissolved. The empire began with iron after the demise of the Greeks and ends with iron when it collapses forever at Christ's return.

History, however, describes the 'demise' of the Roman Empire in the fifth century AD during the reign of Emperor Diocletian. Historians record the reasons for the demise under Diocletian's rule which includes excessive and inequitable taxes, the increase of immigrants to fill the void caused by the expanding military resulting in diluted citizenship, and a shortage of funds to support the military while maintaining roads and buildings. Sound familiar?

But did the Roman Empire really totally and permanently fall?

Approximately 1000 years before Roman Emperor Diocletian ruled, a certain man named Byzas of Megara founded a settlement near the south western shores of the Black Sea. This settlement became known as Byzantium.

This settlement subsequently came under the rule of Media-Persia and then under Alexander the Great. Following Greek rule was the Romans. History reveals that the Roman Empire, after ruling for approximately 700 years, really didn't dissolve but was rather divided into two regions, i.e. the eastern region and the western region.

During the Roman era Byzantium became very popular due to its expanding cultural advancements. While the western region of the Roman Empire continued to decline, the eastern region of Byzantium continued to gain prominence.

Constantine recognized the value of Byzantium and made it the capital of the eastern region of the empire and Byzantium became known as Constantinople.

Beginning in the 7th century AD a new religion came on the scene. This new religion, i.e. Islam, was expanding into Palestine, Syria, and Egypt and posed a threat to Constantinople. Unrest continued for several centuries.

Subsequently in 1453 AD Constantinople, now known as Istanbul, became the capital of the Ottoman Turkish Empire. The Ottoman Turks sided with Germany in WW I and were defeated by allied forces. The previous home of the Islamic Caliphate would then become the Republic of Turkey.

"...The Seven Heads Are Seven Mountains..."

After the defeat and apparent demise of the Ottoman Empire, the new Republic of Turkey was established under the leadership of Mustafa Kemal in 1923.

Kemal's vision for the transformation of the fledgling republic of Turkey included modernization, westernization, and secularization.

This agenda did not set well with many Muslims. The dilution of Islamism with western influence stirred a pious Egyptian Muslim named Hassan al-Banna in 1928 to found what is still known as the Muslim Brotherhood.

In al-Banna's mind it was time to revive the 'Ottoman Empire' and reinstate the Islamic caliphate.

After WW I al-Banna forged relationships with several German and Italian leaders who shared common ideologies. The foundation of the Muslim Brotherhood was greatly influenced by these leaders and ideologies.

The Muslim Brotherhood is presently the largest Muslim organization in the world with many offshoots operating in more than 80 countries.

Three such influential offshoots that are very active in America today include the Council on American Islamic Relations (CAIR), the Organization of Islamic Conference (OIC), and the Muslim Students Association (MSA) just to name a few.

While the republic of Turkey had its origin with westernized aspirations contrary to the agenda of the defeated Ottoman Empire, the present situation appears to be open to change.

Turkey's present Prime Minister, Recep Tayyip Erdogan, is a Muslim. Erdogan raised eyebrows recently when he stated that the term 'moderate Islam' is offensive and that 'Islam is Islam'. Therefore, the future direction of the Republic of Turkey is in question.

According to Islamic literature, however, the future of Turkey has already been determined and recorded centuries ago. Present Islamic author Adnan Oktar (pen name Harun Yahya) sums up numerous Islamic hadiths with these words:

"The establishment of the Turkish-Islamic Union will be the salvation of everyone, of people of all faiths, all nations and all opinions, not just of the Islamic world. This union will bring love, brotherhood, friendship, plenty and abundance to the world.

The Turkish-Islamic Union to be established under Turkish leadership will be instrumental in the world attaining an entirely new beauty…and in the construction of a powerful and deep-rooted civilization.

By Allah's leave, the establishment of the Turkish-Islamic Union is an absolute certainty. This is the destiny ordained by Allah.

One of the main proofs that the Turkish Nation will fulfill this historic responsibility is the way that in the hadith about the end times our Prophet...makes particular reference to Istanbul and to Turkey.

As revealed by the Prophet...Hazrat Mahdi will be active in Istanbul, will construct the Turkish-Islamic Union by bringing the dispersed Turkic states back together..."

Yahya goes on to state, "The foundation of the Turkish-Islamic Union will take place without a drop of blood being spilled..."

To paraphrase Yahya's dissertation, Islam's coming savior will re-establish the Islamic Caliphate in present day Turkey. The caliphate will be re-established peacefully without any bloodshed.

Summarizing, the Roman Empire has really never been dissolved. Its eastern leg survived in the form of Byzantium until 1453 AD when it was overtaken by the Ottoman Turks.

The capital of Constantinople (Istanbul), however, was maintained during the Ottoman reign. The Republic of Turkey subsequently designated Ankara as their capital.

And while the Ottoman Turks were defeated in WW I when they sided with Germany, Islamic literature states that the final Islamic caliphate will be re-established in Turkey under their coming Mahdi, i.e. savior.

Much can be learned by studying Islamic literature relative to Turkey's prominent future.

"...and I saw a woman sitting on a scarlet beast, full of blasphemous names, having seven heads and ten horns." Revelation 17:3

"Here is the mind which has wisdom. The seven heads are seven mountains on which the woman sits, and they are seven kings; five have fallen, one is, the other has not yet come; and when he comes, he must remain a little while. And the beast which was and is not, is himself also an eighth, and is one of the seven, and he goes to destruction." Revelation 17:9-11

Perhaps Islamic prophecy has helped to identify the seventh mountain (kingdom) in the above scripture:

1) Egyptian
2) Assyrian
3) Babylonian
4) Media/Persian
5) Greek
6) Roman
7) Ottoman Turks …Republic of Turkey…Turkish – Islamic Union.

"…The Ten Horns Are Ten Kings…"

According to the Bible the seventh and final gentile kingdom before the return of Christ will consist of ten member nations.

"…and I (John) saw a woman sitting on a scarlet beast… having seven heads and ten horns…and the angel said to me… 'the ten horns which you saw are ten kings, who have not yet received a kingdom, but they receive authority as kings with the beast for one hour. These have one purpose and they give their power and authority to the beast.'" Revelation 17:3, 7, 12-13

Bible students believe the prophet Ezekiel sheds light on the identity of these nations. Let's identify three of them located in different corners of the Fertile Crescent, i.e. Persia (Iran), Libya, and Togarmah (Eastern Turkey). Presently these nations are Islamic and are located in Northern Africa, which is south of Israel, Iran which is east of Israel, and Turkey which is north of Israel.

The ten horns representing the ten member nations of the final gentile kingdom are the same as the ten toes of the image in Nebuchadnezzar's dream.

They are also the same as the ten horns of the fourth great beast in Daniel's dream. Both dreams speak of the federation of nations under the future leader's rule during the prophet Daniel's seventieth week, or seven years.

Recall also that the feet of the image in Nebuchadnezzar's dream had been compromised, i.e. weakened because the iron toes were mixed with clay.

"And in that you saw the feet and toes, partly of potter's clay and partly of iron, it will be a divided kingdom; but it will have in it the toughness of iron...and as the toes of the feet were partly of iron and partly of pottery, so some of the kingdom will be strong and part of it will be brittle."
Daniel 2:41-42

The above passage states the toes themselves are part iron and part clay. That would indicate that some or all of the member nations of that final federation will have compromising ideologies either within themselves or as national entities.

The current uprising in several Islamic nations was/is termed 'Arab Spring'. The naïve believe that the end result will be the toppling of those authoritarian regimes and replaced with democratic governments.

It is also believed by most that the uprisings were/are being spawned by young people demanding an end of oppression. That may have been the beginning spark; however, renowned scholar on Muslim affairs Walid Phares wrote an article entitled, 'Muslim Brotherhood Riding the Crest of Arab Spring'.

The Brotherhood is representing themselves as an unassuming stabilizing force and the answer to the unrest.

Consider further that Turkey's Prime Minister Erdogan was touring Northern Africa's Muslim nations recently and presented Turkey's model as the key for success for those Muslim nations.

This model consists of an Islamic-based political party governing a secular democracy.

If Erdogan's model is adopted in any of these nations it will definitely have the affect of compromise, i.e. iron mixed with clay.

No one can deny that there are exciting times ahead. Our response to that truth should include being informed so each individual can take a stand.

It is helpful to study Islam along with Biblical teachings so as to better understand future prophetic events.

One issue common to both sources of information is that Turkey will definitely have a profound place in future world events.

Three Reasons to 'Talk Turkey'

Previous sections of this chapter have discussed the nation of Turkey relative to the future of the Middle East as it relates to both Israel and America.

The first reason to 'talk Turkey' today is found in Islamic literature. Islam firmly believes that Turkey and Istanbul will once again be the home of the revived Islamic Caliphate.

Recall Islamic author Adnan Oktar summed up numerous Islamic hadiths with the following words:

"The establishment of the Turkish-Islamic Union will be the salvation of everyone, of people of all faiths, all nations and all opinions, not just of the Islamic world.

By Allah's leave, the establishment of the Turkish-Islamic Union is an absolute certainty. This is the destiny ordained by Allah…"

The second reason to 'talk turkey' today is summarized by author and Middle East expert Daniel Pipes. Pipes has studied Turkey and the Middle East for more than four decades and written twelve books of the subject.

He has visited Turkey numerous times; his most recent visit was in December, 2012 and he summarized his finding in an interview with the Turkish press.

Pipes noted that major changes have taken place in Turkey during the 40 years of his study and visits. During the early years of the Republic of Turkey religion was not a primary factor, however, now he sees religion and the acceptance of sharia law slowly gaining a foothold.

When asked about whether Turkey is seen as a power player in the future of the Middle East, he replied:

"Turkey absolutely is the best candidate right now for Middle East leadership. Given its population, the ruling party's vision, its economic strength, and its intellectual capacity, Turkey is the country closest to leading the Middle East."

Pipes notes also that the Republic of Turkey is gradually leaving Western values in favor of Islamism and sharia law.

The third reason to 'talk Turkey' today is found in Biblical prophecy. Ezekiel was told to prophesy against Israel's future enemies.

These enemies of Israel are part of modern day Turkey, Persia (Iran), Ethiopia, and Libya. According to the Bible those nations will suffer profound defeat when they attack Israel.

Of a surety, there are exciting times ahead for the Fertile Crescent. Both the Bible and Islamic literature agree this age will end where civilization began after the flood.

Isn't it a wonderful thing to be able to view history before it happens?

CHAPTER 7

GLIMPSES OF THE FUTURE

The term 'future' in the context of this final chapter includes next year, the end of the current church age, the tribulation period, the millennial kingdom, and the eternal kingdom.

Likewise the term 'glimpses' means only a very small portion of the totality of the future. The following sampling of future Biblical events is by no means intended to be comprehensive. The topics presented represent a broad array of varied future Biblical events.

One major objective is to reveal the inevitable consequences of extrapolating current trends. Another objective is to provide a glimpse of the eternal glory awaiting those who will spend eternity with their Creator.

The chapter will end by acknowledging several tremendously comforting words for those who have been chosen in God before the foundation of the earth, i.e. 'and there will be no more curse' and 'come, Lord Jesus!'

Are America's Greatest Days Ahead?

For those who believe the Bible has neither place nor relevance in America's future, the following might be considered foolishness. However, for those who believe in the sovereignty of God and the validity of the Scriptures, the following will resonate and confirm their perceptions.

A good starting point is to consider the building blocks of this great constitutional republic and compare its foundation with the present. In chapter 4 an example was given about President Obama attempting to apply one of Jesus' parables.

Recall the president touted the proposed benefits of his stimulus program he said his administration could be likened to a wise man who built his house on a rock. The house would not fall because it was founded on the rock.

He was obviously referring to Jesus' parable of the two builders. That is a great scripture; however, the words that provided the context of that passage was omitted.

"Therefore everyone who hears these words of mine and puts them into practice is like a wise man who built his house on the rock." Matthew 7:24

The key to wisdom is not only to hear Jesus' words, but adopt and put them into practice.

Presently nearly 3 out of 4 Americans believe this nation is headed in the wrong direction. Perhaps their thinking is correct, but many if not most believe this nation's problems can be solved with short-term solutions such as an economic recovery.

Then there are those who examine this nation's woes at a deeper level. They examine the policies and ideologies of our leaders that brought us to this point.

Such thinking is more interested in addressing the sources of the problems and changing overall direction.

But flawed ideology is not the only reason for national decline. Study after study confirms that the demographics in the United States are undergoing profound changes.

It is estimated that by 2050 North America and Europe will comprise only 12% of the world's population vs. 28% just a half century ago.

The decline in America's natural growth rate can be attributed to several factors including birth control and abortion. America's immigration policy is partially compensating for the decreased growth rate. One of the challenges of our immigration policy is that many immigrants of today have little or no interest in assimilating into American culture.

Many do not share the same ideals or the religious foundation on which this great nation was founded. America is known for promoting diversity, thus our political correctness accommodates them.

Consider further that nearly a century ago a major portion of immigrants coming to America were from Europe and for the most part welcomed assimilation into American culture. The 'melting pot' has been transformed into multiculturalism. When varied cultures within a nation compete for dominance the end result is a dilution of national values resulting in internal conflict.

Nearly all studies confirm that white America is becoming the minority population segment. Studies also show that white Americans are predominately conservative Christians. As their relative numbers and influence decreases, so grows the gap between what America once was and where she is headed.

Consider Europe and witness their decline. America and other western nations are close behind. Recall that Europe's leaders have recently and collectively warned the rest of the world of the negative affects of their multicultural experiences.

The Bible addresses the issue very succinctly. When God gave Israel the land of Canaan, He gave them instructions and repeated them several times.

"You are to have the same law for the alien and the native-born. I am the LORD your God." Leviticus 24:22

Therefore, Americans can focus on short-term perceived solutions or recognize longer range trends which are unfolding before our eyes and defining our future. However, for the Christian community, the Bible will be consulted to see where America is headed and why.

Can the trends be reversed? Everyone can arrive at their own conclusion. The good news is that regardless of our national destiny every individual can choose their own personal eternal future.

Is America Mentioned in the Bible?

The 'Mother of Harlots' is described in the Bible as the predominant influence on gentile world kingdoms of the past and particularly on the final 10 nation confederation which will be led by the future anti-Christ.

"...There I saw a woman sitting on a scarlet beast that was covered with blasphemous names and had seven heads and ten horns." Revelation 17:3

The final gentile kingdom will, however, turn on the great harlot, according to God's sovereign will, and destroy her.

"The beast and the ten horns you saw will hate the prostitute. They will bring her to ruin and leave her naked...and burn her with fire. For God has put it into their hearts to accomplish his purpose by agreeing to give the beast their power to rule, until God's words are fulfilled." Revelation 17:16-17

The mighty angel then further describes the harlot and the influence she has over the nations' leaders.

"The woman you saw is the great city that rules over the kings of the earth." Revelation 17:18

At this point many attempt to separate chapters 17 and 18 of the Revelation by referring to the woman in chapter 17 as false religion and the focus of chapter 18 being the future world's political, economic, or commercial, system.

However, the text indicates that chapter 18 describes the activities of the woman in chapter 17, i.e. they are one in the same. In other words the woman in chapter 17 is called 'Mother of Harlots' because of what she does in chapter 18. Note the focal point in chapter 18 is also called 'that great city' as is the great harlot in Revelation 17:18 above.

"When the kings of the earth who committed adultery with her and shared her luxury see the smoke of her burning,

they will weep and mourn over her...they will stand far off and cry: 'Woe! Woe, O great city...in one hour your doom has come!'" Revelation 18:9-10

A logical question then arises, i.e. why commerce or materialism would be considered harlotry, or spiritual adultery? An early indication of such a relationship is found in the Old Testament with reference to the ancient city of Nineveh.

"Woe to the city of blood, full of lies, full of plunder...all because of the wanton lust of a harlot, alluring, the mistress of sorceries, who enslaved nations by her prostitution...You have increased the number of your merchants till they are more than the stars of the sky..." Nahum 3:1, 4, 16

A much lengthier and more detailed discussion on commerce and materialism is found in the writings of the prophet Ezekiel. The city cited was Tyre which was known for its international trade associations.

The king of Tyre was energized by Satan himself as was the king of Babylon. The following passages begin with describing Tyre as perfectly situated to be the center of international trade.

"...take up a lament concerning Tyre. Say to Tyre, situated at the gateway to the sea, merchant of peoples on many coasts..." Ezekiel 27:2-3

Next Tyre's trading success is noted and the resulting pride it brings.

"By your wisdom and understanding you have gained wealth for yourself and amassed gold and silver in your treasuries. By your great skill in trading you have increased

your wealth, and because of your wealth your heart has grown proud." Ezekiel 28:4-5

Then Ezekiel notes the king of Tyre was energized by Satan.

"...This is what the Sovereign LORD says: 'You were the model of perfection, full of wisdom and perfect in beauty. You were in Eden, the garden of God...You were blameless in your ways from the day you were created till wickedness was found in you.'" Ezekiel 28:12-13, 15

The king of Tyre then suffers humiliating destruction from God Himself because of his pride and self serving agenda.

"Your heart became proud on account of your beauty, and you corrupted your wisdom because of your splendor. So I threw you to the earth; I made a spectacle of you before kings." Ezekiel 28:17

Now with that abbreviated introduction relative to commerce and materialism, how does that relate to the future judgment of that great 'city' Babylon, and more specifically America?

The key to understanding the scriptural ramifications of commerce in Revelation is determined by purpose and motive. Note the common ground in each of the following verses.

"For all the nations have drunk the maddening wine of her adulteries. The kings of the earth committed adultery with her, and the merchants of the earth grew rich from her excessive luxuries." Revelation 18:3

"Give her as much torture and grief as the glory and luxury she gave herself. In her heart she boasts, 'I sit

as queen; I am not a widow, and I will never mourn.'" Revelation 18:7

Note in the above verse the harlot considers herself to be a queen and not a widow. Could it be that she has been deceived by not being aware of her gross harlotries, i.e. her spiritual adulteries embodied in commerce and materialism?

"When the kings of the earth who committed adultery with her and shared her luxury see the smoke of her burning, they will weep and mourn over her." Revelation 18:9

It becomes clear that the focus of chapter 18 is the abundance of spiritual adultery committed by the kings of the earth as they strive to increase riches for the purpose of living luxuriously.

The word 'luxury' has profound multiple meanings. In the King James Version the word used is 'delicacy'. The Greek base for both in the present context means wantonness or lasciviousness. It represents an insatiable desire for personal pleasure to the extent such desire overrides restraint or reason.

The primary thought is the focus on the present, or short term gratification with little concern for the future.

"Do not store up for ourselves treasures on earth...But store up for yourselves treasures in heaven, where moth and rust do not destroy...For where your treasure is, there your heart will be also." Matthew 6:19-21

"Command those who are rich in this present world not to be arrogant nor to put their hope in wealth, which is so uncertain, but to put their hope in God, who richly provides us with everything for our enjoyment."

1 Timothy 6:17

The desire towards self and present fulfillment along with its underlying motives was succinctly described by the Apostle John.

"Do not love the world or anything in the world. If anyone loves the world, the love of the Father is not in him. For everything in the world – the cravings of sinful man, the lust of his eyes and the boasting of what he has and does – comes not from the Father but from the world." 1 John 2:15-16

Spiritual adultery is simply forsaking God's word and instructions, ignoring His provisions, and giving priority to the pursuit of 'things' present. Instead of seeking God, men will trade around the world to find fulfillment.

The terms merchant and/or merchandise is found six times in the 18th chapter of Revelation. The consequence of placing priority on 'things' before God is clearly spelled out.

" Woe! Woe, O great city, dressed in fine linen, purple and scarlet, and glittering with gold, precious stones and pearls! In one hour such great wealth has been brought to ruin..." Revelation 18:16

How does this relate to America, if in fact it does at all?

"...Your merchants were the world's great men. By your magic spell all the nations were led astray." Revelation 18:23b

"A second angel followed and said, 'Fallen! Fallen is Babylon the Great, which made all the nations drink the maddening wine of her adulteries.'" Revelation 14:8

Every individual can determine for themselves if 'all' in the above includes America, or if America would never be involved in forsaking God for the pursuit of 'things' and present self-fulfillment.

Most Americans agree that America is on an 'unsustainable' path but there is little agreement on the reasons.

It was obvious that the tone of the 2012 presidential election echoed the infamous slogan coined by James Carville in 1992 describing Bill Clinton's campaign.

'It's the economy, stupid!'

Transparency…Someday

It seems like every presidential candidate vows that if elected their administration will be the most transparent in history. President Obama certainly made that claim. Most likely he was referring to one of Webster's definitions of transparency namely 'free from pretense or deceit'.

On the other hand the opposite of transparency includes clandestine conduct of which one would be ashamed. Synonyms include secret, hidden, or concealed. History will reveal which definition best suits this president.

Transparency is also a popular Biblical teaching in both Old and New Testaments. The major premise is that one cannot take a secret to the grave thinking it will never be revealed.

Biblical synonyms for transparency include reveal, uncover, unveil, disclose and open. In the present age many trial lawyers earn their living by circumventing or suppressing the truth. Consider the numerous congressional hearings being conducted regarding the numerous 'phony scandals' surrounding this current administration's activities.

Millions of dollars and untold hours are being spent, again just to arrive at the truth. And then there is the use of the Fifth Amendment where a person is exempted from testifying if their testimony would be self incriminating.

The above is just a sampling of the games being played during this present age. The truth, however, is already known and is being stored in a data base that would put the National Security Agency to shame. And all will be revealed in due time.

The doctrine of 'openness' and transparency was taught by Jesus beginning with the parable of the lamp.

"For whatever is hidden is meant to be disclosed, and whatever is concealed is meant to be brought out into the open." Mark 4:22

Note the wording 'hidden…and whatever is concealed.' There is no such thing as a 'delete' button in God's data base.

Jesus then taught that all types of hypocrisy would be exposed.

"There is nothing concealed that will not be disclosed, or hidden that will not be made known. What you have said in the dark will be heard in the daylight, and what you have whispered in the ear in the inner rooms will be proclaimed from the roofs." Luke 12:2-3

Recall that the Pharisees were the prime examples of hypocrites. They pretended to be righteous when in fact Jesus exposed them as being of their father, the devil.

Paul carried on with the concept of openness and total transparency. He taught that even the supposed inner thoughts of the heart would be exposed in due time.

"Therefore judge nothing before the appointed time; wait till the Lord comes. He will bring to light what is hidden in darkness and will expose the motives of men's hearts..." 1 Corinthians 4:5

Solomon, who was considered to be the wisest man in the world during the days of the kings, summarized the Old Testament teachings of transparency.

"Now all has been heard; here is the conclusion of the matter: Fear God and keep his commandments, for this is the whole duty of man. For God will bring every deed into judgment, including every hidden thing, whether it is good or evil." Ecclesiastes 12:13-14

At the end of the recent trial of Jodi Arias she made the now infamous statement: 'Death is the ultimate freedom.'

Perhaps many share her thinking, however, those who find themselves before the great white throne will learn the truth of the matter.

"Then I saw a great white throne and him who was seated on it. Earth and sky fled from his presence, and there was no place for them. And I saw the dead, great and small, standing before the throne..." Revelation 20:11-12

Signs of the Times

The Biblical plan for the future is laid out in detail. The sequence of events is plainly seen, but what is not clear is the timing of the end of the present age. Jesus admonished

His disciples to be watchful for the signs pointing to His return.

"Now learn this lesson from the fig tree: As soon as its twigs get tender and its leaves come out, you know that summer is near. Even so, when you see all these things, you know that it is near, right at the door."

Matthew 24:32-33

This present time period will be one of accelerated confusion and deceit. Recall that deceit is the attempt to draw one away from the truth and the truth is embodied in Christ. Because of the presence of deceit, lawlessness will abound.

"...and many false prophets will appear and deceive many people. Because of the increase of wickedness (lawlessness), the love of most will grow cold..." Matthew 24:11-12

A synonym for lawlessness in the New Testament is transgression. It is broader than just dismissing the 'rule of law' established by men. It means to transgress the 'divinely instituted law' of God.

"Everyone who sins breaks the law; in fact, sin is lawlessness."

1 John 3-4

In other words, a sign of the times is to diminish the focus on Godly things. Furthermore, those who cling to the truth and Godly things will be despised.

"Then you will be handed over to be persecuted and put to death, and you will be hated by all nations because of me." Matthew 24:9

The Apostle and teacher Paul wrote that lawlessness had already begun in the early days of the church. The early days of the church marked the beginning of this present age.

"For the secret power of lawlessness is already at work..."

2 Thessalonians 2:7

Not only is lawlessness present in this age, it will accelerate until it is personified in the anti-Christ.

"...this is the last hour; and as you have heard that the antichrist is coming, even now many antichrists have come. This is how we know it is the last hour." 1 John 2:18

Many Christians are beginning to associate any religion that is contrary to John's teachings relative to Christ and antichrist with lawlessness.

During this present time period emotions will run hot and will crescendo towards the end of the period.

"At that time many will turn away from the faith (be offended) and will betray and hate each other, and many false prophets will appear and deceive many people." Matthew 24:10-11

While this verse appears less dramatic than wars and earthquakes, it does paint a picture of man's relationships with each other during this time period.

The term 'offend' means to set a trap or cause one to stumble and fall. 'Betray' is to deliver to the power and pleasure of one's enemies, while 'hate' means to persecute and/or cause tribulation. Deception is the impetus for such hatred because truth is rejected. The persecution of Christians will definitely increase during this present age as will anti-Semitism.

The Bible states that the major events spoken by Jesus in the gospel records relative to the current age are just the beginning.

"Nation will rise against nation, and kingdom against kingdom. There will be famines and earthquakes in various places. All these are the beginning of birth pains." Matthew 24:7-8

When such birth pains begin, they increase and continue until the birth.

Many will rely on America's resiliency and power to deliver her from the events spoken of in the Bible. Each individual has the right to assess the future from their own vantage point.

While many will take God's justice lightly, there are many who will accept Biblical teachings by faith, and then there are many who will review Israel's history to shed light and credibility on Biblical prophecy.

It is always interesting to examine current events, political climate, and contemporary societal issues to see how the present age compares with 2,000 year old writings as future history continues to unfold.

Ignoring Warning Signs

Most people that profess Christianity and embrace the Bible believe that the primary attribute of God is love. In fact perhaps the single best known and quoted verse in the Bible is:

"For God so loved the world that he gave his one and only Son, that whoever believes in him shall not perish but have eternal life." John 3:16

The above verse was written by the Apostle John. This same John wrote the Gospel of John, three epistles bearing his name, and the final book of the Bible, i.e. The Revelation of Jesus Christ.

One might think that the final book of the Bible would sum up the love of God. It really does because it reveals that He will remove the curse on the earth; however, the primary focus of The Revelation is to reveal and describe the single most pronounced attribute of God, which is that above all things He is just. That means all things must be made right according to His eternal word.

Interestingly in The Revelation the word love/loved is found six times. The word wrath is found twelve times, the word judge/judgment is found fourteen times, and the word kill/killed is found sixteen times.

God's wrath is required because He is just. Wrath is from the Greek word *orge*. This wrath includes anger with grief. God's required wrath is divine judgment executed with grief.

If man would take God at His word, as most claim that they do, then His wrath is seen to be inevitable. Throughout the Bible consequences for certain choices are outlined in detail.

The wrath of God was introduced in the Bible prior to the Book of Revelation.

"But because of your stubbornness and your unrepentant heart, you are storing up wrath against yourself for the day of God's wrath, when his righteous judgment will be revealed. God 'will give to each person according to what he has done.'" Romans 2:5-6

America's Vision vs. God's Standard of Justice

Consider that on September 11, 2001 the United States was attacked by Islamist terrorists. The loss of life on that terrible day approached 3,000 people. Shortly thereafter the Department of Homeland Security was established with the hopes of preventing any such future attacks.

On December 26, 2004 an earthquake registering 9.0 occurred off Indonesia's Sumatra Island that triggered a tsunami that killed upwards of 300,000 people. Now the United Nations is pushing for a tsunami early warning system for the Indian Ocean similar to that covering the Pacific Ocean.

In these two examples the people in America and Indonesia suffered catastrophic events and then set out to prevent their reoccurrence, or at least mitigate the effect of such occurrences.

Throughout the Bible there are examples of divine retribution to nations, including Israel, due to disobeying God's instructions. The simple fact is that if one believes the Bible that God is sovereign over all things, one must also believe that God has the sovereign right to establish the rules of conduct and see that they are followed. If man desires to 'go it on his own', then he must be willing to risk the consequences of his independent choices.

And so it is, America lost nearly 3,000 innocent lives on 9-11 and the Indonesia tsunami took nearly 300,000 lives. The Book of Revelation reveals that during the seven year tribulation period that is approaching there will be more than 3.0 billion lives lost. That means that for every single life lost during the 2004 tsunami, there will be 10,000 lives lost during the tribulation period.

"...and there before me was a pale horse! Its rider was named Death, and Hades was following close behind him. They were given power over a forth of the earth to kill..."
Revelation 6:8

The present population of the earth is estimated at approximately 7.0 billion, therefore, the above verse represents approximately 1.75 billion people. Unknown, however, is the population of Christians who will have been removed. Then consider:

"... 'Release the four angels who are bound at the great river Euphrates.' And the four angels who had been kept ready for this very hour and day and month and year were released to kill a third of mankind."
Revelation 9:14-15

Add another 1.75 billion so the total number of those killed thus far is 3.5 billion. We can't overlook two other verses that tells about more death but doesn't give a number.

"The third angel sounded his trumpet, and a great star, blazing like a torch, fell from the sky on a third of the rivers and on the springs of water...and many people died from the waters that had become bitter."
Revelation 8:10-11

Many would say that God is a God of love and mercy and He could simply overlook all of man's errors and forget about the tribulation. The truth is that He can't do that because He is just. All wrongs must be made right.

Therefore, while God is a loving God and He is merciful, His predominant attribute, and in fact His very nature, is that He is just. So not all will taste of God's mercy, but all will taste of His justice. But let it not be overlooked that according to the Bible, those who will not receive God's mercy have chosen to reject it and 'do it their way'.

This great truth is not pleasant to many who would just as soon avoid hearing about it; however, Jesus addressed that very issue:

"I warn everyone who hears the words of the prophecy of this book: If anyone adds anything to them, God will add to him the plagues described in this book. And if anyone takes words away from this book of prophecy, God will take away from him his share in the tree of life..."
Revelation 22:18-19

The very fact that the Revelation was written nearly two thousand years ago proves that man is too preoccupied with his own agenda to give more than lip service to the prophecies contained therein.

In other words, the great tribulation is a done deal. We have chosen to ignore the warning signs.

War on Christian Extremism Far From Over

The war against Christian extremism is in fact accelerating. Reports reveal that over 100,000 Christians are killed annually just because they are Christian. The Christian Brotherhood is monitoring closely those countries in which these deaths occur.

Another parallel term for 'Christian extremism' would be 'Christian radicalism'. Christians are considered radical/extreme because they are willing to give their lives for their faith instead of seeking to kill those who don't share that faith.

In other words, Christians do not kill for their faith; rather they are killed for their faith.

"This is how we know what love is: Jesus Christ laid down his life for us. And we ought to lay down our lives for our brothers." 1 John 3:16

Christians obey the Bible which teaches that God will take vengeance on those who persecute them in His manner and His time.

According to the Bible hatred towards Christians will increase and the killing of believers will peak during the future 7 year tribulation period.

"...And I saw the souls of those who had been beheaded because of their testimony for Jesus and because of the word of God. They had not worshiped the beast or his image and had not received his mark..."

Revelation 20:3

There are numerous professing Christians who really do not posses 'saving faith' and the time will come when they will abandon their profession when they realize the true cost of following Christ.

"They went out from us, but they did not really belong to us. For if they had belonged to us, they would have remained with us; but their going showed that none of them belonged to us." 1 John 2:19

Recall that there is no such thing as a 'moderate Christian'.

The biggest enemy of the Christian Brotherhood is all around and practically goes unchallenged and for the most part unnoticed. It is political correctness. This subtle enemy manifests itself whenever Christian values and Bible teachings are compromised or marginalized for the sake of pacifying the few.

It is indeed a sad commentary that this present administration is setting the culture for marginalizing Christianity in America. Likewise, such contemporary thinking is totally at odds with Scriptural teachings. The major emphasis appears to be appeasing the growing progressive movement in this country.

Persecution of the Christian Brotherhood is most often exemplified in the doctrine of 'Modern Day Pharisees'. And again, the Obama administration is more concerned with appeasing such adherents than challenging their incompatible religious/political views.

Jesus warned repeatedly and forcefully to stand up to this group and rebuke them in total. And again, this anti-Christian philosophy is all around us.

The Obama administration reeks with hypocrisy. On the one hand they preach the doctrine of the separation of church and state while on the other hand they do not speak out against the modern day Pharisaic viewpoint which does not even to pretend to recognize such a separation.

Many Kingdoms Will Become a Single Kingdom

The term 'kingdom' in both Old and New Testaments implies sovereign rule, reign, or dominion over a people by a single monarch, i.e. a king.

In the prophecy of Daniel the rise and fall of various world kingdoms is described. King Nebuchadnezzar had a dream which troubled him but he wouldn't reveal the dream to his magicians, astrologers, or sorcerers. His thinking was that if he revealed his dream they would devise their private interpretation just to pacify him.

The young Hebrew lad Daniel, however, not only revealed the dream but also interpreted it for the king. The dream described the rise of the Babylonian kingdom and the other world kingdoms that would follow through the ages. The dream ended with the total destruction of these kingdoms and the inauguration of God's Kingdom.

"In the time of those kings, the God of heaven will set up a kingdom that will never be destroyed, nor will it be left to another people. It will crush all those kingdoms and bring them to an end, but it will itself endure forever...The dream is true and the interpretation is trustworthy."

Daniel 2:44-45

Several centuries earlier the prophet Isaiah had announced the King who would fulfill Nebuchadnezzar's dream.

"For to us a child is born, to us a son is given, and the government will be on his shoulders...He will reign on David's throne and over his kingdom, establishing and upholding it with justice and righteousness from that time on and forever." Isaiah 9: 6-7

During the early days of His earthly ministry Jesus taught His disciples to pray that God's kingdom would come to earth in due time.

"This, then, is how you should pray: 'Our Father in heaven, hallowed be your name, your kingdom come, your will be done on earth as it is in heaven." Matthew 6:9-10

However, the Jews thought that He would establish His prophesied kingdom while He was presently on earth.

They didn't realize that the 'kingdom' over which Christ would reign would be a Spiritual kingdom to begin with, but would become physical and visible at a later time.

The kingdom that Jesus ushered in during His lifetime is referred to in the Bible as the Kingdom of Heaven, or the Kingdom of God.

"Once, having been asked by the Pharisees when the kingdom of God would come, Jesus replied, 'The kingdom of God does not come with your careful observation... because the kingdom of God is within you.'"

Luke 17:20-21

When Pilate interrogated Jesus as to whether He was King of the Jews Jesus did in fact acknowledge that He was a King but He further stated at that time His kingdom was presently not of this world.

At the return of Christ to end the great tribulation, the kingdoms of the world will be defeated by Christ and His physical kingdom will be established to fulfill Nebuchadnezzar's dream and Isaiah's prophecy.

The Apostle John vividly describes the scene in the final book of the Bible.

"The seventh angel sounded his trumpet, and there were loud voices in heaven, which said: 'The kingdom of the world has become the kingdom of our Lord and of his Christ, and he will reign for ever and ever."

Revelation 11:15

Recall Daniel's words spoken 600 years before the birth of Christ, i.e. 'the dream is certain, and its interpretation is sure.'

Wars of the Future

The Bible states there will be wars throughout the present age. The disciples asked Jesus for a sign that would indicate when He would return to earth and Jesus replied:

"You will hear of wars and rumors of wars, but see to it that you are not alarmed...Nation will rise against nation, and kingdom against kingdom..."

Matthew 24:6-7

Jesus said that between the time of His ascension to heaven and the time that He returns to earth wars would be ongoing along with famines, pestilences, and earthquakes. These would be just samples of what is to come.

In particular, there will be three major wars that will occur in the future. The third and final war will end all wars.

The first major future war will occur at the beginning of the seven year tribulation period.

"And there was war in heaven. Michael and his angels fought against the dragon, and the dragon and his angels fought back. But he was not strong enough, and they lost their place in heaven. The great dragon was hurled down – that ancient serpent called the devil, or Satan, who leads the whole world astray. He was hurled to the earth, and his angels with him."

Revelation 12:7-9

"...But woe to the earth and the sea, because the devil has gone down to you! He is filled with fury, because he knows that his time is short."

Revelation 12:12

Satan's permanent abode in heaven ended ages ago, but he still has access to the throne to accuse God's people.

However, his access to the throne of God after losing his permanent abode in Heaven is confirmed in the Book of Job.

"One day the angels came to present themselves before the LORD, and Satan also came with them. The LORD said to Satan, 'Where have you come from?' Satan answered the LORD, 'From roaming through the earth and going back and forth in it.'" Job 1:6-7

The second of the three major future wars will occur at the end of the seven year tribulation period. This war will in fact end the tribulation. This war occurs when Christ returns to earth to claim and rule over that which He paid for on the Cross.

"A day of the LORD is coming...I will gather all the nations to Jerusalem to fight against it...Then the LORD will go out and fight against those nations..." Zechariah 14:1-3

"Then they gathered the kings together to the place that in Hebrew is called Armageddon." Revelation 16:16

"I saw heaven standing open and there before me was a white horse, whose rider is called Faithful and True. With justice he judges and makes war." Revelation 19:11

"Then I saw the beast and the kings of the earth and their armies gathered together to make war against the rider on the horse and his army...But the beast was captured, and with him the false prophet...the two of them were thrown alive into the fiery lake of burning sulfur. The rest of them

were killed with the sword that came out of the mouth of the rider on the horse..." Revelation 19:19-21

After the second war at the end of the tribulation period the nations will be disarmed, neither will nation fight against nation anymore.

"In the last days the mountain of the LORD's temple will be established...and all nations will stream to it... The law will go out from Zion, the word of the LORD from Jerusalem. He will judge between the nations...They will beat their swords into plowshares and their spears into pruning hooks. Nation will not take up sword against nation, nor will they train for war anymore." Isaiah 2:2-4

One war remains after this. Recall at the end of the tribulation period Satan is not destroyed as are the Anti-Christ and false prophet, but is bound in the bottomless pit for a thousand years.

"And I saw an angel coming down out of heaven, having the key to the Abyss and holding in his hand a great chain. He seized the dragon, that ancient serpent, who is the devil, or Satan, and bound him for a thousand years. He threw him into the Abyss, and locked and sealed it...to keep him from deceiving the nations anymore until the thousand years were ended."

Revelation 20:1-3

"When the thousand years are over, Satan will be released from his prison and will go out to deceive the nations in the four corners of the earth...to gather them to battle. In number they are like the sand on the seashore. They marched across the breadth of the earth and surrounded the camp of God's people...But fire came down from heaven

and devoured them. And the devil, who deceived them, was thrown into the lake of burning sulfur, where the beast and the false prophet had been thrown. They will be tormented day and night for ever and ever." Revelation 20:7-10

That is the third and final of the major wars to come. This final war will be very brief and the rebellious of the nations will be devoured by fire from heaven. God Himself is the ultimate victor. The battle of good vs. evil has been won!

The Jesus Everyone Will Know

For many people the person of Jesus is learned through history, i.e. His birth, life, death, resurrection, and ascension. But according to the Bible everyone will experience Him personally in the future.

The death of Jesus is commemorated and His resurrection celebrated during the time known as 'Easter' which correctly translated means Passover. Therefore, let's begin at that point.

"And being found in appearance as a man, he humbled himself and became obedient to death – even death on a cross! Therefore God exalted him to the highest place and gave him the name that is above every name, that at the name of Jesus every knee should bow, in heaven and on earth and under the earth, and every tongue confess that Jesus Christ is Lord, to the glory of God the Father." Philippians 2:8-11

The above exemplifies the humanity of Jesus and His original earthly mission. However, His humanity is just one necessary aspect of His being. He is also unquestionably deity.

"He is the image of the invisible God, the firstborn over all creation. For by him all things were created: things in heaven and on earth visible and invisible, whether thrones or powers or rulers or authorities..."

Colossians 1:15

"For in Christ all the fullness of the Deity lives in bodily form..."

Colossians 2:9

The most succinct expression of His deity is found in the gospel of John.

"I and the Father are one." John 10:30

The Bible clearly states that one does not know Jesus if both aspects of His being are not embraced, i.e. His humanity and His deity.

"Many deceivers, who do not acknowledge Jesus Christ as coming in the flesh, have gone out into the world. Any such person is the deceiver and the antichrist...Anyone who runs ahead and does not continue in the teaching of Christ does not have God; whoever continues in the teaching has both the Father and the Son." 2 John 7, 9

Therefore, if anyone denies Jesus as the Passover Lamb of God, i.e. His humanity and His first earthly mission of death on the cross, or if anyone denies the deity of Jesus, that person in reality does not have God at all. In fact the primary purpose of deceivers is to cause one to deny one or both aspects of Jesus the Christ.

But what Jesus has done in the past as recorded in history is just the beginning. Jesus of the future will turn the world upside down upon returning to earth.

Forty days after Jesus' resurrection He ascended to heaven which was witnessed by His disciples.

"After he said this, he was taken up before their very eyes, and a cloud hid him from their sight. They were looking intently up into the sky as he was going, when suddenly two men dressed in white stood beside them... they said, 'why do you stand here looking into the sky? This same Jesus, who has been taken from you into heaven, will come back in the same way you have seen him go into heaven.'" Acts 1:9-11

So while just his disciples witnessed His ascension, the entire world will witness His return at a time not revealed in the Scriptures. Jesus described His return.

"For as lightning that comes from the east is visible even in the west, so will be the coming of the Son of Man... At that time the sign of the Son of Man will appear in the sky, and all the nations of the earth will mourn. They will see the Son of Man coming on the clouds of the sky, with power and great glory." Matthew 24:27, 30

Much more is revealed about Jesus in the final book of the Bible, i.e. the Revelation. Specifically this final book is the Revelation of Jesus Christ.

The word 'revelation' is from the Greek *apokalupsis* meaning not only to unveil, but also to explain that which is unveiled.

Those who know God by embracing both the humanity and deity of Jesus will greatly rejoice at His return. However, those who are living on earth at His return and have left Jesus either in the manger or in the grave and are not willing to change 'will seek death and will not find it.'

The return of Jesus to earth is the fulfillment of prophecy penned centuries before His birth.

"In my vision at night I looked, and there before me was one like a son of man, coming with the clouds of heaven... He was given authority, glory and sovereign power; all peoples, nations and men of every language worshiped him. His dominion is an everlasting dominion that will not pass away, and his kingdom is one that will never be destroyed." Daniel 7:13-14

Without question, we are headed for some very exciting times! It causes one to wonder if our personal as well as our national priorities are in line with the known future.

What Will Redeemed Man do in the Future?

The 'future' in this section begins with the return of the redeemed with Christ after the tribulation period which marks the beginning of Christ's millennial reign in Jerusalem.

One thing is certain, redeemed man in the future will not be idle. Many New Testament teachings describe 'on the job training' for the future.

There is little question that we presently live in a litigious society. Everyone is passionate about preserving his/her rights. Paul teaches that those chosen for the kingdom (Biblical saints) should be able to settle differences between themselves during the present age without resorting to the legal system for adjudication.

"If any of you has a dispute with another, dare he take it before the ungodly for judgment instead of before the saints? Do you not know that the saints will judge the

world? And if you are to judge the world, are you not competent to fudge trivial cases? Do you not now that we will judge angels? How much more the things of this life!" 1 Corinthians 6:1-3

The Bible also teaches that Jesus' disciples would participate in the administration of Israel in the future.

"Jesus said to them, 'I tell you the truth, at the renewal of all things, when the Son of Man sits on his glorious throne, you who have followed me will also sit on twelve thrones, judging the twelve tribes of Israel.'" Matthew 19:28

Paul summarized the concept of shared reign with Christ:

"...if we endure, we will also reign with him. If we disown him, he will also disown us." 2 Timothy 2:12

Another significant aspect of the future is that there will be no marriage relationships.

"Jesus replied, 'The people of this age marry and are given in marriage. But those who are considered worthy of taking part in that age and in the resurrection from the dead will neither marry nor be given in marriage, and they can no longer die...'" Luke 20:34-36

Earlier in man's odyssey God sanctioned marriage for several specific purposes including populating the earth and exercising dominion over it.

"So God created man in his own image...male and female he created them. God blessed them and said to them, 'Be fruitful and increase in number; fill the earth and subdue it. Rule over...every living creature that moves on the ground.'" Genesis 1:27-28

In the renewed earth and New Jerusalem there will be a fixed number of occupants determined from the foundation of the world who will live forever so there will be no need for marriage and procreation.

During the millennial period there will be ample opportunities for those who enjoying fishing.

"...and I saw water coming out from under the threshold of the temple...water that was ankle-deep. He measured off another thousand cubits and led me through water that was knee-deep. He measured off another thousand and led me through water that was up to the waist. He measured off another thousand, but now it was a river that no one could cross...There will be large numbers of fish, because this water flows there and makes the salt water fresh... fishermen will stand along the shore...The fish will be of many kinds..." Ezekiel 47:1, 3-5, 9-10

God never intended man to be idle either in this life or in the future. God created man to be productive. Such was true in the Garden of Eden before sin and there is no indication that redeemed man will be idle in the ages to come. Adam was very productive in the original Garden.

"The LORD God took the man and put him in the Garden of Eden to work it and take care of (tend, cultivate) it." Genesis 2:15

The Hebrew 'tend' is synonymous with 'dress' meaning to serve, till, and/or plow while the Hebrew 'keep' likewise means to work or toil.

When Jesus was resurrected, He was raised in His new glorified, immortal body. And recall Jesus was/is the firstfruits of the harvest.

Therefore, all justified mankind, i.e. those redeemed from the curse pronounced in Genesis chapter 3, will be raised in like fashion as their Redeemer.

"Dear friends, now we are children of God, and what we will be has not yet been made known. But we know that when he appears, we shall be like him, for we shall see him as he is." 1 John 3:2

"But our citizenship is in heaven. And we eagerly await a Savior from there, the Lord Jesus Christ, who... will transform our lowly bodies so that they will be like his glorious body." Philippians 3:20-21

"...in a flash, in the twinkling of an eye, at the last trumpet. For the trumpet will sound, the dead will be raised imperishable, and we will be changed. For the perishable must clothe itself with the imperishable, and the mortal with immortality." 1 Corinthians 15:52-53

Not only will the redeemed be raised with immortal bodies, they will be granted extra-human wisdom and understanding.

"Now we see but a poor reflection as in a mirror; then we shall see face to face. Now I know in part; then I shall know fully, even as I am fully known." 1 Corinthians 13:12

The Bible further reveals that each individual will be different. Recall what the Apostle John said previously…'it has not yet been revealed what we shall be…'

"But someone may ask, 'How are the dead raised? With what kind of body will they come?' How foolish! What you sow does not come to life unless it dies. When you sow, you do not plant the body that will be, but just a seed, perhaps of wheat or of something else. But God gives it a body as

he has determined, and to each kind of seed he gives its own body."

1 Corinthians 15:35-38

"The creation waits in eager expectation for the sons of God to be revealed...Not only so, but we ourselves, who have the firstfruits of the Spirit, groan inwardly as we wait eagerly for our adoption as sons, the redemption of our bodies." Romans 8:19, 24

The future redeemed will also be given extra-human powers similar to the resurrected Christ. They will not be restricted to time and other physical dimensions and limitations.

The inheritance of the redeemed is beyond description.

"However, as it is written: 'No eye has seen, no ear has heard, no mind has conceived what God has prepared for those who love him.'"

1 Corinthians 2:9

What a glorious future for those who take God at His word. The hope of the redeemed will be realized when faith in that which cannot be seen is seen.

Things We Know...

The future of the earth and mankind has already been determined and documented.

Inasmuch as man was created in God's own image man will live eternally. There are two basic divisions of all mankind, i.e. those in the majority who have disobeyed God and refused redemption, and those in the minority who have disobeyed God but accepted His gracious gift of redemption.

There is no such thing as cessation of being for any man.

Likewise the earth will also endure forever; however, the earth will be redeemed and renewed from the consequences of the fall in the Garden of Eden and the subsequent curse.

"Generations come and generations go, but the earth remains forever."

Ecclesiastes 1:4

"He set the earth on its foundations; it can never be moved."

Psalm 104:5

"The highest heavens belong to the LORD, but the earth he has given to man." Psalm 115:16

When God prepared the earth for man, He appointed him to have dominion over all other living creatures.

After the fall of Adam in the Garden of Eden, God in mercy and longsuffering began to implement His plan of redemption foreordained before the foundation of the world. He would insure that man would fulfill the purpose for which he was created and nothing could thwart that plan.

History has confirmed time and again that God's redemptive plan is right on schedule.

The Kingdom of God is presently invisible in the midst of the highly visible and physical kingdoms of the world.

Future steps in God's plan include Christ removing the 'church' so God can deal with national Israel and the rest of unrepentant mankind during the seven year tribulation period.

At the end of the tribulation Christ will return to earth, separate the goats from the sheep and the invisible Kingdom of God will become totally visible as Christ will rule the nations for 1000 years from His throne in earthly Jerusalem.

The goats will be banished to eternal punishment while the sheep will be ushered into the kingdom prepared for them 'from the foundation of the world.'

The timing of Christ's return has also been precisely planned but not revealed.

"No one knows about that day or hour, not even the angels in heaven, nor the Son, but only the Father." Mark 13:32

The 1000 year kingdom is a major milestone towards the eternal new heaven and new earth. All forms of human government will have failed including democracy as well as capitalism. Only the saved will enter the kingdom. All others have been banished and Israel's enemies will have been destroyed.

But God's testing of man isn't complete until the end of the 1000 year kingdom when Satan is released from the bottomless pit to tempt all who were born in the flesh during the millennium.

After Satan's final defeat the earth will receive her new face and be adorned for her intended purpose which is to be the eternal dwelling place for redeemed man.

At that time all existing elements which are known by their atomic weights will be dissolved and all matter will be made new. The new elements will not be subject to decay, as in the present law of physics known as half-life, but will last throughout eternity.

"But the day of the Lord will come like a thief. The heavens will disappear with a roar; the elements will be

destroyed by fire, and the earth and everything in it will be laid bare...But in keeping with his promise we are looking forward to a new heaven and a new earth, the home of righteousness." 2 Peter 3:10, 13

"Then I saw a new heaven and a new earth for the first heaven and the first earth had passed away..." Revelation 21:1

In both Hebrew and Greek the meaning of the word 'new' is considered to be renew, a superior creation on the original physical object such as noted in the following:

"Therefore, if anyone is in Christ, he is a new creation; the old has gone, the new has come." 2 Corinthians 5:17

A Christian is considered a new creation. During this age the Christian is renewed in spirit, however, he is still consigned to his original body.

The promise of a new heaven and earth was introduced in the Old Testament.

"Behold, I will create new heavens and a new earth. The former things will not be remembered, nor will they come to mind. But be glad and rejoice forever in what I will create, for I will create Jerusalem to be a delight and its people a joy." Isaiah 65:17-18

"As the new heavens and the new earth that I make will endure before me, declares the LORD, so will your name and descendants endure." Isaiah 66:22

After the sin plagued earth has passed away the new earth will appear. Christ will have completed His earthly mission.

"Then the end will come, when he hands over the kingdom to God the Father after he has destroyed all

dominion, authority and power. For he must reign until he has put all his enemies under his feet. The last enemy to be destroyed is death...When he has done this, then the Son himself will be made subject to him who put everything under him, so that God may be all in all." 1 Corinthians 15:24-28

Recall Christ's mission.

"...The reason the Son of God appeared was to destroy the devil's work." 1 John 3:8b

And then there are the beautiful, powerful and most comforting words in the Bible.

"No longer will there be any curse..." Revelation 22:3a

The certainty of Biblical prophecy should cause all to pause and consider whether priorities both as individuals as well as a nation are in sync with the known future.

Or will the earth's inhabitants be like those in the time of Noah and the flood.

"For in the days before the flood, people were eating and drinking, marrying and giving in marriage, up to the day Noah entered the ark; and they knew nothing about what would happen until the flood came and took them all away. That is how it will be at the coming of the Son of Man."

Matthew 24:36-39

The world is oblivious to the future undisputable judgment, just as it was prior to the flood.

Christians, however, with anticipation and great joy focus on the final words of the Bible.

"He who testifies to these things says, 'Yes, I am coming soon.' Amen. Come, Lord Jesus." Revelation 22:20

"The grace of the Lord Jesus be with God's people. Amen."
Revelation 22:21